# The American C

'There can be no doubt abou[...]
back in touch with his best s[...]
American Dream, and back on top of his talent.' *New
York Times*

Miller's latest play offers a cross-section of American
society during the first four years of the Great Depression, showing people of all classes waiting for 'the
dream to come back from wherever it had gone to'.
*The American Clock* shows 'the same kind of writing
that made *Death of a Salesman* a masterpiece'. Clive
Barnes, *New York Post*

Published alongside its British premiere, this is the
first new Miller play to be staged in Britain for thirteen
years.

*The photograph on the front cover shows William Ather-
ton and Joan Copeland in a scene from the New York
production of* The American Clock. *Both this and the
photograph of Arthur Miller on the back cover are by
Inge Morath and are reproduced by permission of
Magnum Photos, Inc.*

Arthur Miller

# The American Clock

METHUEN · LONDON

First published in the USA in 1982 by the Dramatists Play
Service Inc.
First published in Great Britain in 1983 simultaneously in hard-
back and as a Methuen Paperback by Methuen London Ltd.,
11 New Fetter Lane, London EC4P 4EE

Printed by Richard Clay (The Chaucer Press) Ltd,
Bungay, Suffolk

TO INGE AND REBECCA

# NOTE ON PRODUCTION

*The American Clock* was first produced at the Harold Clurman Theatre, in New York City, and opened at the Spoleto Festival's Dockside Theatre in Charleston, South Carolina, on May 24, 1980, directed by Dan Sullivan.

It opened at the Biltmore Theatre in New York on November 20, 1980, under the direction of Vivian Matalon. The scenery was designed by Karl Eigsti; the lighting was by Neil Peter Jampolis; and the costumes were by Robert Wojewodski. The cast, in order of appearance, was as follows:

| | |
|---|---|
| LEE BAUM | William Atherton |
| MOE BAUM | John Randolph |
| CLARENCE, WAITER, ISAAC, JEROME, PIANO MOVER | Donny Burks |
| ROSE BAUM | Joan Copeland |
| FRANK, LIVERMORE, MAN IN WELFARE OFFICE, STANISLAUS | Ralph Drischell |
| GRANDPA, KAPUSH | Salem Ludwig |
| FANNY MARGOLIES, MYRNA | Francine Beers |
| CLAYTON, SIDNEY MARGOLIES, RALPH DURANT, SHERIFF, PIANO MOVER, TOLAND | Robert Harper / Alan North |
| TONY, TAYLOR, DUGAN | Edward Seamon |
| WAITER, BICYCLE THIEF, RUDY, PIANO MOVER, RYAN | Bill Smitrovich |
| JOE, BUSH | David Chandler |
| DORIS, ISABEL, GRACE | Marilyn Caskey |
| IRENE | Rosanna Carter |
| JEANETTE RAMSEY, EDIE, LUCILLE, ATTENDANT | Susan Sharkey |

# CHARACTERS

ARTHUR ROBERTSON
CLARENCE, *a shoeshine man*
LEE BAUM
MOE BAUM, *Lee's father*
ROSE BAUM, *Lee's mother*
FRANK, *the Baum's chauffeur*
FANNY MARGOLIES, *Rose's sister*
GRANDPA, *Rose's father*
DR ROSMAN
WILLIAM DURANT ⎤
JESSE LIVERMORE ⎬ *financiers*
ARTHUR CLAYTON ⎦
TONY, *a speakeasy owner*
WAITER
DIANA MORGAN
HENRY TAYLOR, *a farmer*
MRS TAYLOR, *his wife*
HARRIET, *their daughter*
CHARLEY
JUDGE BRADLEY
BREWSTER
FRANK HOWARD, *auctioneer*
SIDNEY MARGOLIES, *Fanny's son*
DORIS GROSS, *the landlady's daughter*
JOEY, *a boyhood friend*
RALPH ⎤
RUDY ⎬ *students*
ISABEL, *a prostitute*
RYAN, *supervisor of a federal relief office*
MATTHEW R. BUSH ⎤
GRACE
KAPUSH
DUGAN ⎬ *people at the relief office*
IRENE
TOLAND
LUCY ⎦
EDIE, *a comic strip writer*
LUCILLE, *Rose's niece*
STANISLAUS, *a seaman*

ISAAC, *a lunch-counter proprietor*
SHERIFF
FARMERS
DEPUTIES
PIANO MOVERS

This version of *The American Clock* was used as the basis of the Birmingham Repertory Theatre's production in 1983.

# Act One

*The set is a flexible area for actors. The few pieces of furniture required should be openly carried on by the actors. An impression of a surrounding vastness should be given, as though the whole country were really the setting, even as the intimacy of certain scenes is provided for. The background can be sky, clouds, space itself, or an impression of the United States' geography.*

*Light rises on* LEE BAUM *who enters and faces the audience. In his fifties, greying hair, wears tweed jacket and has a vaguely preppy look, a journalist.*

LEE. There have been only two American disasters that were truly national. Not the first or second World Wars, Vietnam or even the Revolution. Only the Civil War and the Great Depression touched nearly everyone wherever they lived and whatever their social class. (*Slight pause.*) Personally, I believe that deep down we are still afraid that suddenly, without warning, it may all fall apart again. And that this fear, in ways we are rarely conscious of, still underlies every ... (ARTHUR ROBERTSON *has entered. In his seventies, a corporate leader. In blue blazer, white turtle neck, white shoes, carrying a cane. Tends to grin ironically.*)

ROBERTSON. Sorry, but I don't think that kind of collapse is really possible again. And I don't mean only the stock market. I mean the emotional collapse. By the year 1929 you had a general belief that every

American was inevitably going to get richer every year. People are a lot more sophisticated now, they expect ups and downs, they are much more sceptical . . .

LEE. Is it scepticism or a deep fear that the whole thing can suddenly cave in and that nothing is really under control?

ROBERTSON. Well whatever it is you can always get out of the way if you use your head. I made more money in the Depression than I ever had before. And I think it's interesting why I wasn't destroyed by the Crash. In 1927 – the height of the boom – I read that the Wright Aeronautical Company was building the plane that would take Lindbergh across the Atlantic. I bought Wright stock, and in one morning it went up sixty-seven points. That was the day I ceased to believe in the permanency of the boom. Only an illusion can multiply itself sixty-seven times in three hours, and I began to remove myself from the market. In two years, it was lying all over the floor. (ROSE BAUM *appears, softly playing the piano, a romantic light on her.*)

LEE (*the sight of her moves him*). But there were people who could not pull out because they believed. And with all their hearts. For them the clock would never strike midnight, the dance and the music could never stop . . .

ROBERTSON (*recalling, mournfully*). Oh, I know, yes – the Believers. (CLARENCE, *a black shoeshine man enters, sets his box down. As* ROBERTSON *approaches him,* LEE *moves in another direction towards* ROSE.) How you making out, Clarence? (*Puts his shoe up on the box and slipping off his grey wig, tosses it offstage – he is in his forties.*)

ROSE (*to* LEE). Sing, Darling!

*Tossing his greying wig offstage, and with a boyish air*

... LEE *sings first line of 'For I'm just a vagabond lover . . .' Blackout on* ROSE *and* LEE.

CLARENCE (*taking bill from his pocket*). Mr Robertson, I like to lay another ten dollars on that General Electric. You do that for me? (*Hands bill to* ROBERTSON.)

ROBERTSON. How much stock you own now, Clarence?

CLARENCE. Well, that ten ought to buy me a thousand dollars' worth, so altogether I guess I got me about hundred thousand dollars in stock.

ROBERTSON. And how much cash you got home?

CLARENCE. Oh, I guess about forty, forty-five dollars.

ROBERTSON (*slight pause*). All right, Clarence, let me tell you something. But I want you to promise me not to repeat it to anyone.

CLARENCE. I never repeat a tip you give me, Mr Robertson.

ROBERTSON. This isn't quite a tip, this is what you might call an un-tip. Take all your stock, and sell it.

CLARENCE. Sell! Why just this morning in the paper Mr Andrew Mellon say the market's got to keep goin' up. *Got* to!

ROBERTSON. I have great respect for Andrew Mellon, Clarence, but he's up to his eyebrows in this game – he's got to say that. You sell, Clarence, believe me.

CLARENCE (*drawing himself up*). I never like to criticise a customer, Mr Robertson, but I don't think a man in your position ought to be carryin' on that kind of talk! Now you take this ten, sir, put it on General Electric for Clarence.

ROBERTSON. I tell you something funny, Clarence.

CLARENCE. What's that, sir?

ROBERTSON. You sound like every banker in the United States.

CLARENCE. Well I should hope so!

ROBERTSON. Yeah, well ... good-bye. (*He goes.* CLA-RENCE *takes his shoeshine box off. Light rises on* ROSE *at the piano, dressed for an evening out. She plays 'Vagabond Lover' softly. Two valises stand centre stage.*)

LEE (*glances at* ROSE *as he removes jacket and pulls ups his trousers to make knickers of them*). Lindbergh had flown the Atlantic because he believed; Babe Ruth kept smashing home runs because he believed; a tremendous broad-shouldered woman named Gertrude Ederle swam the English Channel and Charley Paddock, the World's Fastest Human, won a race against a racehorse – because he believed – and one afternoon my mother came home and she had bobbed her beautiful long hair in which I had always believed. (ROSE *sings the opening line of 'Vagabond Lover'.* LEE *tries to join in but his voice is quavering. She stops.*)

ROSE. What's the matter with you? (*He can only shake his head – 'nothing'.*) Oh, for God's sake! Nobody's going to bother with long hair anymore. All I was doing was winding it up and winding it down ...

LEE. It's *okay*! I just didn't think it would ever ... happen!

ROSE. But why can't there be something new!

LEE. But why didn't you *tell* me?

ROSE. Because you would do exactly what you're doing now! – Carrying on like I was some kind of I-don't-know-what! Now stop being an idiot and *sing*. (LEE *starts the song again. Spoken.*) You're not breathing, dear. (MOE *enters in tuxedo, carrying a phone.*)

MOE. Trafalgar five, seven-seven-one-one. (*He joins them in the song.* FRANK, *in chauffeur's uniform, enters, applauding.*)

ROSE. Rudy Vallee is turning green.

MOE (*in phone*). Herb? I'm just thinking maybe I ought

to pick up another five hundred shares of General
Electric – good. (*Hangs up.*)

FRANK. Car's ready, Mr Baum.

ROSE (*to* FRANK). You'll drop us at the theatre and then
take my father and sister to Brooklyn and come back
for us after the show. And don't get lost please.

FRANK. No, I know Brooklyn. (*He goes off with the bag-
gage.* FANNY *enters –* ROSE's *sister, with four walking
sticks and two hat boxes.*)

FANNY (*apprehensively*). Rose ... listen ... Papa really
doesn't want to move. (*A slow turn with rising eyebrows
from* MOE; ROSE *is likewise alarmed.*)

ROSE (*to Fanny*). Don't be silly, he's been here six
months.

FANNY (*fearfully, voice lowered*). I'm telling you ... he
is not happy about it.

MOE (*resoundingly understating the irony*). He's not
happy.

FANNY (*to* MOE). Well, you know how he loves space,
and this apartment is so roomy.

MOE (*to* LEE). He bought himself a grave, you know, it's
going to be in the cemetery on the aisle. So he'll have a
little more room to move around ...

ROSE. Oh, stop it.

MOE. ... Get in and out quicker.

FANNY. Out of a grave?

ROSE. He's kidding you, for God's sake!

FANNY. Oh! (*To* ROSE.) I think he's afraid my house'll
be too small; you know, with the girls and Sidney and
us and the one bathroom. And what is he going to do
with himself in Brooklyn? He never liked the country.

ROSE. Fanny, dear – make up your mind – he's going to
love it with you.

MOE. Tell you, Fanny – maybe we should *all* move over

to your house and he could live here with eleven rooms
for himself and we'll send the maid every day to do his
laundry . . .

FANNY. He's brushing his hair, Rose, but I know he's
not happy. I think what it is, he still misses Mama, you
see.

MOE. Now *that's* serious – a man his age still misses his
mother . . .

FANNY. No, *our* mother – *Mama*. (*To* ROSE, *almost
laughing, pointing at* MOE.) He thought Papa misses his
own mother!

ROSE. No he didn't, he's kidding you!

FANNY. Oh you . . .! (*She swipes at* MOE.)

ROSE (*walking her to the doorway*). Go, hurry him up. I
don't want to miss the first scene of this show, it's
supposed to be wonderful.

FANNY. See, what it is, something is always happening
here, but in our house it's . . . very *quiet*, you
know? . . .

MOE (*in phone*). . . . Trafalgar five, seven-seven-one-one.

FANNY. . . . I mean with the stock market and the business . . . Papa just loves all this! (GRANDPA *appears.
Suit, cane, overcoat on arm. Very neat, proper – and
very sorry for himself. Comes to a halt, already hurt.*
FANNY, *deferentially.*) You ready, Papa?

MOE (*to* GRANDPA). See you again soon, Charley! (*On
phone.*) Herb? . . . Maybe I ought to get rid of my
Worthington Pump. Oh . . . thousand shares? And
remind me to talk to you about gold will you? – Good.

FANNY (*with* ROSE, *getting* GRANDPA *into his coat*).
Rose'll come every few days, Papa . . .

ROSE. Sunday we'll all come out and spend the day.

GRANDPA. Brooklyn is full of tomatoes.

FANNY. Not so much anymore, you'd be surprised.

They're starting to put up big apartment houses now; it's practically not the country anymore. (*Happy reassurance.*) On some streets there's hardly a tree! (*To* ROSE, *of her diamond bracelet.*) I'm looking at that bracelet! Is it new?

ROSE. For my birthday.

FANNY. It's gorgeous.

ROSE. He gave exactly the same one to his mother.

FANNY. She must be overjoyed.

ROSE (*with a cutting smile to* MOE). Why not?

GRANDPA (*a sudden despairing announcement*). Well? So I'm going! (*Shaking his head disapprovingly, as he starts off.*)

LEE. Bye-bye, Grandpa!

GRANDPA (*goes to* LEE, *offers his cheek, gets his kiss, then pinches* LEE's *cheek*). You be a good boy. (*He strides past* ROSE, *huffily snatches his hat out of her hand, and goes out.*)

MOE. There goes the boarder. I lived to see it!

ROSE (*to* LEE). Want to come and ride with us?

LEE. I think I'll stay and work on my radio.

ROSE. Good, and go to bed early. I'll bring home all the music from the show and we'll sing it tomorrow. (*Kisses.*) Good night, darling. (*She has a fur stole over her arm and swings out.*)

MOE (*to* LEE). Whyn't you get a haircut?

LEE. I did, but it grew back, I think.

MOE (*realising* LEE's *size*). Should you talk to your mother about college or something?

LEE. Oh no, not for a couple of years.

MOE. Oh. Okay, good. (*He laughs and goes out, perfectly at one with the world.* ROBERTSON *appears and walks over to an armless couch and lies down.* DR ROSMAN *appears and sits in a chair behind* ROBERTSON's *head.*)

ROBERTSON. Where'd I leave off yesterday?

DR ROSMAN. Your mother had scalded the cat. (*Pause.*)

ROBERTSON. There's something else, Doctor. I feel a conflict about saying it . . .

DR ROSMAN. That's what we're here for.

ROBERTSON. I don't mean in the usual sense. It has to do with money.

DR ROSMAN. Yes?

ROBERTSON. Your money.

DR ROSMAN (*turns down to him alarmed*). What about it?

ROBERTSON (*hesitates*). I think you ought to get out of the market.

DR ROSMAN. Out of the market!

ROBERTSON. Sell everything.

DR ROSMAN (*pauses. Raises his head to think, speaks carefully*). Could you talk about the basis for this idea? When was the first time you had this thought?

ROBERTSON. About four months ago. Around the middle of May.

DR ROSMAN. Can you recall what suggested it?

ROBERTSON. One of my companies manufactures kitchen utensils.

DR ROSMAN. The one in Indiana.

ROBERTSON. Yes. In the middle of May all our orders stopped coming.

DR ROSMAN. Completely?

ROBERTSON. Dead stop. It's now the end of August and they haven't resumed.

DR ROSMAN. How is that possible? The stock keeps going up.

ROBERTSON. Thirty points in less than two months; this is what I've been trying to tell you for a long time now, Doctor – the market represents nothing but a state of mind. (*Sitting up.*) On the other hand, I must face the possibility that this is merely my personal fantasy . . .

DR ROSMAN. Yes, you've always had a fear of approaching disaster.

ROBERTSON. But I've had meetings at the Morgan Bank all week and it's the same in almost every industry – the warehouses are overflowing, we can't move the goods, that's an objective fact.

DR ROSMAN. Have you told your thoughts to your colleagues?

ROBERTSON. They won't listen. Maybe they can't afford to – we've been tossing the whole country on to a crap table in a game where nobody is ever supposed to lose . . .! I sold off a lot two years ago but when the market opens tomorrow I'm cashing in the rest. I feel guilty for it, but I can't see any other way.

DR ROSMAN. Why does selling make you feel guilty?

ROBERTSON. Dumping twelve million dollars in securities could start a slide. It could wipe out thousands of widows and old people . . . I've even played with the idea of making a public announcement.

DR ROSMAN. But that could start a slide in itself, couldn't it?

ROBERTSON. But it would warn the little people.

DR ROSMAN (*with mounting anxiety*). But . . . you might end up responsible for a collapse.

ROBERTSON. But knowing what I know, and saying nothing, I'm responsible too, aren't I?

DR ROSMAN. Yes, but selling out quietly might not disturb the market quite so much. You *could* be wrong, too.

ROBERTSON. I suppose so. Yes . . . Maybe I'll just sell and shut up. You're right. I could be mistaken.

DR ROSMAN (*relieved*). You probably are. – But I think I'll sell out anyway.

ROBERTSON. Fine, Doctor. (*Stands.*) And one more thing. This is going to sound absolutely nuts, but . . . when you get your cash, don't keep it. Buy gold.

DR ROSMAN. You can't be serious.

ROBERTSON. Gold bars, Doctor. The dollar may disappear with the rest of it. (*Extends his hand.*) Well, good luck.

DR ROSMAN. Your hand is shaking.

ROBERTSON. Why not? If they heard this there aren't two great bankers in the United States who wouldn't agree that Arthur A. Robertson had lost his mind. – Gold bars, Doctor . . . and don't put them in the bank. In the basement. Take care now. (*He goes. Then* ROSMAN. *Light rises on Tony's Speakeasy. An offstage orchestra is playing the latest hit, waiters are setting the table where two stately men in evening clothes take chairs, drinking their brandy. Now* LEE *enters observing all this. – He once again is in his grey wig.*)

LEE. Ah yes, the Great Men. (ROBERTSON *enters. He too is grey now.*)

ROBERTSON (*chuckling*). Oh indeed – the legendary Jesse Livermore, the genius of corporate finance, William Durant . . .

LEE. When I think of how we idolised these gurus who were nothing but pickpockets in a crowd of pilgrims . . .

ROBERTSON. Yes, but they too believed.

LEE. Oh what did they believe!

ROBERTSON. Why, they believed in the most important thing of all – that nothing is real! That if it was Monday and you wanted it to be Friday, and enough people could be made to believe it *was* Friday – then by God it was Friday! In fact, had they really been cynical, they and the country would have been a lot better off!

LIVERMORE. Tony?

TONY (*entering*). Yes, Mr Livermore? Little more brandy, Mr Durant?

LIVERMORE. About Randolph Morgan. Could you actually see him falling?

TONY. Oh yeah. It was still that blue light, just before it gets dark? And I don't know why, something made me look up. And there's a man flyin' spread-eagle, falling through the air. He was right on top of me, like a giant! (*Looks down.*) And I look. I couldn't believe it. It's Randolph!

LIVERMORE. Poor, poor man.

DURANT. Damned fool.

LIVERMORE. I don't know – I think there is a certain gallantry . . . When you lose other people's money as well as your own, there could be no other way out.

DURANT. There's always a way out. The door.

LIVERMORE (*raising his glass*). To Randolph Morgan. (DURANT raises his glass.)

TONY. Amen here. And I want to say something here – everybody should get down on their knees and thank John D. Rockefeller.

LIVERMORE. Now you're talking.

TONY. Honest to God, Mr Livermore, didn't that shoot a thrill in you? I mean there's a *man* – to come out like that with the whole market falling to pieces and say, 'I and my sons are buying six million dollars in common stocks.' I mean that's a bullfighter.

LIVERMORE. He'll turn it all around, too.

TONY. Sure he'll turn it around, because the man's a capitalist, he knows how to put up a battle. You wait, tomorrow morning it'll all be shootin' up again like Roman candles! (*Enter waiter, who whispers in* TONY's *ear.*) Sure, sure, bring her in. (*Waiter hurries out.* TONY *turns to financiers.*) My God, it's Randolph's sister . . . she don't know yet. (*Enter* DIANA.) How do you do, Miss Morgan, come in, come in. Here, I got a nice table for you.

DIANA (*the bright Southern belle*). Thank you!

TONY. Can I bring you nice steak? Little drink?

DIANA. I believe I'll wait for Mr Robertson.

TONY. Sure. Make yourself at home.

DIANA. Are you the . . . *famous* Tony?

TONY. That's right, miss.

DIANA. I certainly am thrilled to meet you. I've read all about this marvellous place. (*Looking about avidly.*) Are all these people literary?

TONY. Well not all, Miss Morgan.

DIANA. But this is the speakeasy F. Scott Fitzgerald frequents, isn't it?

TONY. Oh yeah, but tonight is very quiet with the stock market and all, people stayin' home a lot the last couple days.

DIANA. Is that gentleman a writer?

TONY. No, miss, that's Jake the Barber, he's in the liquor business.

DIANA. And these? (*Points to* DURANT *and* LIVERMORE. DURANT, *having overheard, stands.*)

TONY. Mr Durant, Miss Morgan. Mr Livermore, Miss Morgan.

DIANA. Not *the* Jesse Livermore?

LIVERMORE. Afraid so, yes!

DIANA. Well I declare! – And sitting here just like two ordinary millionaires! This is certainly a banner evening for me! – I suppose you know Durham quite well.

LIVERMORE. Durham? I don't believe I've ever been there.

DIANA. But your big Philip Morris plant is there. – You do still own Philip Morris, don't you?

LIVERMORE. Oh yes, but to bet on a horse there's no need to ride him. I never mix in business, I am only interested in stocks.

DIANA. Well that's sort of miraculous, isn't it, to own a place like that and never've seen it! My brother's in brokerage – Randolph Morgan?

LIVERMORE. I dealt with Randolph when I bought the controlling shares of IBM. Fine fellow.

DIANA. But I don't understand why he'd be spending the night in his office. The market's closed at night, isn't it? (*Both men shift uneasily.*)

DURANT. Oh yes, but there's an avalanche of selling orders from all over the country, and they're working round the clock to tally them up. The truth is, there's not a price on anything at the moment. In fact, Mr Clayton over there at the end of the bar is waiting for the latest estimates.

DIANA. I'm sure something will be done, won't there? (*Laughs.*) They've cut off our telephone!

LIVERMORE. How's that?

DIANA. I don't actually know – it seems that Daddy's lived on loans the last few months and his credit stopped, I had no idea! (*Laughs.*) I feel like a figure in a dream. I sat down in the dining car, absolutely famished, and realised I had only forty cents! I am surviving on chocolate bars! (*Her charm barely hiding anxiety.*) Whatever has become of all the money?

LIVERMORE. You mustn't worry, Miss Morgan, there'll soon be plenty of money. Money is like a shy bird: the slightest rustle in the trees and it flies for cover. But money cannot bear solitude for long, it must come out and feed. And that is why we must all speak positively and show our confidence. With Rockefeller's announcement this morning the climb has probably begun already. (CLAYTON *appears in the dim periphery with phone to his ear.*)

DURANT. If I were you, Miss Morgan, I would prepare myself for the worst.

LIVERMORE. Now, Bill, there is no good in that kind of talk!

DURANT. It's far more dreamlike than you imagine, Miss Morgan. Here I am chatting away while that gentleman at the end of the bar, that gentleman who has just put down the telephone, is undoubtedly steeling himself to tell me that I have lost control of General Motors.

DIANA. What! (ARTHUR CLAYTON *has indeed put down the phone, straightened his waist-coat, and is now crossing to their table.*)

DURANT (*watching him approach*). If I were you, I'd muster all the strength I have, Miss Morgan. (CLAYTON *comes to a halt before* DURANT.) Yes, Clayton? (TONY *enters, sets a glass of wine before* DIANA.)

CLAYTON. If we could talk privately, sir ... (TONY *glances knowingly at* CLAYTON, *goes.*)

DURANT. Am I through?

CLAYTON. If you could borrow for two or three weeks –

DURANT. From whom?

CLAYTON. I don't know, sir.

DURANT (*stands*). Good night, Miss Morgan. (*She is looking up at him, astonished.*) How old are you?

DIANA. Nineteen.

DURANT. I hope you will look things in the face, young lady. Shun paper. Paper is the plague. Good luck to you. (*He turns to go.*)

LIVERMORE. We have to talk, Bill ...

DURANT. Nothing to say, Jesse. Go to bed, old boy, it's long past midnight. (*He goes.*)

LIVERMORE (*turns to* CLAYTON, *adopting a tone of casual challenge*). Clayton . . . what's Philip Morris going to open at, can they tell?

CLAYTON. Below twenty. No higher. If we can find buyers at all.

LIVERMORE (*his smile gone*). But Rockefeller, Rockefeller . . .

CLAYTON. It doesn't seem to have had any effect, sir. (LIVERMORE *stands. Pause.*) I should get back to the office, sir, if I may. (LIVERMORE *is silent.*) I'm very sorry, Mr Livermore. (CLAYTON *goes.* DIANA *sees the excruciating look coming on to* LIVERMORE'*s face, and half stands.*)

DIANA. Mr Livermore? . . . (ROBERTSON *enters, in his forties now.*)

ROBERTSON. Sorry I'm late, Diana – how was the trip? (*Her expression turns him to* LIVERMORE. *He goes to him.*) Bad, Jesse?

LIVERMORE. I am wiped out, Arthur.

ROBERTSON (*trying for lightness*). Come on now, Jesse, a man like you has always got ten million put away somewhere.

LIVERMORE. No – no. I always felt that if you couldn't have *real* money, might as well not have any. Is it true what I've heard, that you sold out in time?

ROBERTSON. Yes, Jesse. I told you I would.

LIVERMORE (*slight pause*). Arthur, can you lend me five thousand dollars?

ROBERTSON. Certainly. (*Sits, removes one shoe.*)

LIVERMORE. What the hell are you doing? (ROBERTSON *removes a layer of five-thousand-dollar bills from the shoe, hands* LIVERMORE *one as he stands.* LIVERMORE *stares down at* ROBERTSON'*s shoes*.) By God. Don't you believe in anything?

ROBERTSON. Not much.

LIVERMORE. Well, I suppose I understand that. (*Folds the bill.*) But I can't say that I admire it. (*Pockets the bill. Looks down again at* ROBERTSON'*s shoes and shakes his head.*) Well, I guess it's your country now. (*He turns like a blind man and goes out.*)

ROBERTSON. Five weeks ago, on his yacht in Oyster Bay, he told me he had four hundred and eighty million dollars in common stocks.

DIANA (*turning to him from staring after* LIVERMORE). Is Randolph ruined too?

ROBERTSON (*takes her hand*). Diana ... Randolph is dead. (*Both hands fly to her cheeks.*) He ... fell from his window. (*Diana stands, astonished, seeing. All fade, except* ROBERTSON, *in spotlight, who turns front to audience.*)

ROBERTSON. Not long after, Mr Livermore sat down to a good breakfast in the Sherry-Netherland Hotel, and calling for an envelope addressed it to Arthur Robertson, inserted a note for five thousand dollars, went into the washroom, and shot himself. (*Light on* LEE, *as he rides in on a bike.*) How did an event like that strike you, out there in Brooklyn? Did it disturb your faith in the system at all?

LEE. Oh no, at that stage I didn't know there was a system. I thought that if a man was – say, like my father – hard-working and making the right goods, he got to be well-off. That's all. Life was a question of individuals, I think.

ROSE (*calling from offstage*). Lee?

ROBERTSON. Interesting. (*He walks into darkness as* ROSE *appears.*)

ROSE (*a small paper bag in her hand*). I want you to do something – oh, what a beautiful bike!

LEE. It's a Columbia Racer! I just bought it from Georgie Rosen for twelve dollars.

ROSE. Where'd you get twelve dollars?

LEE. I emptied my savings account. But it's worth way more! . . .

ROSE. Well I should say! – Listen, darling, you know how to get to Third Avenue and Nineteenth Street, don't you?

LEE. Sure, in ten minutes.

ROSE (*lifts out a diamond bracelet from bag*). This is my diamond bracelet. (*Reaches into bag and brings out a card.*) And this is Mr Sanders' card and the address. He's expecting you; just give it to him and he'll give you a receipt.

LEE. Is he going to fix it?

ROSE. No, dear. It's a pawnshop. Go, I'll explain sometime.

LEE. Can't I have an idea? What's a pawnshop?

ROSE. Where you leave something temporarily and they lend you money on it, with interest. I'm going to leave it the rest of the month, till the market goes up again. I showed it to him on Friday and we're getting a nice loan on it.

LEE. But how do you get it back?

ROSE. You just pay back the loan plus interest. But things'll pick up in a month or two. Go on, darling, and be careful! I'm so glad you bought that bike . . . it's gorgeous!

LEE (*mounting his bike*). Does Papa know?

ROSE. Yes, dear. Papa knows . . . (*She starts out when* JOEY *hurries on.*)

JOEY. Oh, hya, Mrs Baum.

ROSE. Hello, Joey . . . did you get thin?

JOEY. Me? – (*Touches his stomach defensively.*) No, I'm okay. (*To* LEE *as well – as he takes an eight-by-ten photo out of envelope.*) See what I just got? (ROSE *and* LEE *look at the photo.*)

ROSE (*impressed*). Where did you get that!

LEE. How'd you get it autographed?

JOEY. I just wrote to the White House.

LEE (*running his finger over the signature*). Boy . . . look at that, huh? – 'Herbert Hoover'!

ROSE. What a human thing for him to do! – What did you write him?

JOEY. Just wished him success . . . you know, against the Depression.

ROSE (*wondrously*). Look at that! – You're going to end up a politician, Joey. (*Returns to studying the photo.*)

JOEY. I might, I like it a lot . . .

LEE. But what about dentistry?

JOEY. Well, either one.

ROSE. Get going, darling. (*She goes, already preoccupied with the real problem.* LEE *mounts his bike . . .*)

LEE. You want to shoot some baskets later?

JOEY. What about now?

LEE (*embarrassed*). No . . . I've got something to do for my mother. Meet you on the court in an hour . . . (*Starts off.*)

JOEY (*stops him*). Wait, I'll go with you, let me on! (*Starts to mount the crossbar.*)

LEE. I can't, Joey.

JOEY (*sensing some forbidden area, surprised*). Oh!

LEE. See you on the court. (LEE *rides off.* JOEY *examines the autograph and mouths silently . . .* 'Herbert Hoover'. *Shakes his head proudly and walks off.* FRANK *appears in chauffeur's cap and overcoat and in mime dusts off a*

*large limousine with a cloth from his pocket, blowing on a*
*spot here and there. Carries a folded laprobe under one*
*arm.* MOE *enters, stylishly dressed in fur-collared over-*
*coat.*)

FRANK. Morning, Mr Baum. Got the car nice and
warmed up for you this morning, sir. And I had the
laprobe dry cleaned.

MOE (*hands* FRANK *a bill*). What is that, Frank?

FRANK. Oh. Looks like the garage bill.

MOE. What's that about tyres on there?

FRANK. Oh yes, sir, this is the bill for the new tyres last
week.

MOE. And what happened to those tyres we bought six
weeks ago?

FRANK. Those weren't very good, sir, they wore out
quick. And I want to be the first to admit that.

MOE. But twenty dollars apiece and they last six weeks?

FRANK. That's just what I'm telling you, sir – they were
just no good. But these ones are going to be a whole lot
better, though.

MOE. Tell you what, Frank . . .

FRANK. Yes, sir. – What I mean, I'm giving you my personal guarantee on this set, Mr Baum.

MOE. I never paid no attention to these things, but maybe
you heard of the market crash? – The whole thing
practically floated into the ocean, y'know.

FRANK. Oh yes, sir, I certainly heard about it.

MOE. I'm glad you heard about it because I heard a *lot*
about it. In fact, what you cleared from selling my tyres
over the last ten years –

FRANK. Oh no, sir! Mr Baum!

MOE. Frank, lookin' back over the last ten years, I never
heard of that amount of tyres in my whole life, since I
first come over from Europe a baby at the age of six.

That is a lot of tyres, Frank; so I tell ya what we're gonna do now, you're going to drive her over to the Pierce Arrow showroom and leave her there, and then come to my office and we'll settle up.

FRANK. But how are you going to get around!

MOE. I'm a happy man in a taxi, Frank.

FRANK. Well I'm sure going to be sorry to leave you people.

MOE. Everything comes to an end, Frank, it was great while it lasted. No hard feelings. (*Shakes* FRANK's *hand*.) Bye-bye.

FRANK (*all his uniformed stature suddenly gone*). But what . . . what am I supposed to do now?

MOE. You got in-laws?

FRANK. . . . But I never got along with them.

MOE. You should've. (*Hurrying off, calling* . . .) Taxi! (FRANK, *cap in hand, starts to walk aimlessly;* ROBERTSON *now appears, again in his seventies, and stares into* FRANK's *face as he walks past and goes*.)

ROBERTSON (*gravely*). They just walked away . . . to nothing; no unemployment insurance, no social security, just fresh air. About that time I made a deal with a Negro chap who worked in my building – every night around six he'd line up seventy-five people and I'd march them into the Mcfadden Penny Restaurant, so-called, where you could buy a fair meal for seven cents. There were seventy-five new ones every night. It began to look like Germany in 1922 . . . and I worried about the banks. There were times I walked around with as much as twenty-five, thirty thousand dollars in my shoes. (LEE *has entered, pushing an armchair loaded with a small table and phone which he sets up*.)

LEE. The population jumped on that block – married children coming back home to live, parents moving back with their children . . . babies were crying where there hadn't been a baby in twenty years . . .

ROBERTSON. There you go, you see? – it revived the family. Progress through catastrophe! (*He and* LEE *go off in opposite directions as* GRANDPA *enters, carrying four or five walking sticks. He comes to a point and lays them on the floor. He is also carrying two hatboxes by their strings; he puts them down and sits in the chair, looking peevish.* ROSE *enters, carrying an unfolded bed-sheet, wearing a house-dress, energetically at work.*)

ROSE (*sees the walking sticks on the floor*). What are you doing?

GRANDPA (*a final verdict*). There's no room for these in my closet . . .

ROSE. For a few *canes*?

GRANDPA. And what about my hats? – You shouldn't have bought such a small house, Rose.

ROSE (*starts to leave*). I'll be right down. (*Of the canes.*) I'll put them in the front-hall closet.

GRANDPA. No, I don't want them where they fall down, people step on them. – And where will I put my hats?

ROSE (*trying not to explode*). Papa, what do you want from me? We are doing what we can do!

GRANDPA. One bedroom for so many people is not right – you had three bathrooms in the apartment and you used to look out the window, there was the whole New York. Here . . . listen to that street out there, it's a Brooklyn cemetery. And this barber is *very* bad – Look what he did to me. (*Shows her.*)

ROSE. Why? It's beautiful. (*Brushes hairs straight.*) It's just a little uneven . . .

GRANDPA (*pushing her hand away*). I don't understand, Rose – why does he declare bankruptcy if he's going to turn around and pay his debts?

ROSE. For his reputation.

GRANDPA. His reputation! He'll have the reputation of a fool! – The reason to go bankrupt is *not* to pay your debts!

ROSE (*uncertain herself*). He wanted to be honourable.

GRANDPA. But the whole beauty of it is you don't have to pay anybody. He should've asked me. When I went bankrupt I didn't pay *nobody*!

ROSE (*deciding*). I've got to tell you something, Papa . . .

GRANDPA. And you'll have to talk to Lee – he throws himself around in his bed all night, wakes me up ten times, and he leaves his socks on the floor . . . (*Raises a foot to make a step.*) . . . I have to step over them.

ROSE. I don't want Moe to get aggravated, Papa. (*He is reached, slightly glances at her*). He might try to start a new business, so he's nervous.

GRANDPA. What did I say?

ROSE. Nothing. (*He remorsefully helps her to fold up the sheet. She suddenly embraces him, then glances at the canes.*) Maybe I can find an umbrella stand someplace.

GRANDPA. I was reading about this Hitler . . .

ROSE. I was just thinking before, when Mama used to stand in front of the mirror, her face was so fine, she looked like a China doll.

GRANDPA. . . . He's chasing all the radicals out of Germany. He wouldn't be so bad if he wasn't against the Jews. He won't last six months . . . Reminded me years ago when I used to take Mama to Baden-Baden this time of year . . .

ROSE. How beautiful she was.

GRANDPA. . . . One time we were sitting on the train ready to leave for Berlin. And suddenly a man gallops up calling out my name. So I says, 'Yes, that's me!' And through the window he hands me my gold watch and chain – 'You left it in your room, mein Herr.' Such a thing could only happen in Germany. This Hitler is finished.

ROSE. Please ... (*Of the canes.*) Put them back in your closet, heh? (*She starts to leave.*)

GRANDPA. All I said was if he's declaring bankruptcy, then he –

ROSE. I don't want him to get mad, Papa! (*She cuts her rebellion short and loads him with canes and his hatboxes.*)

GRANDPA (*mutters*). Man don't even know how to go bankrupt. (*He goes off.* LEE *appears on his bike – but dressed now for winter. He dismounts, parks the bike just as* ROSE *lies back in the chair.*)

LEE. Ma! Guess what!

ROSE. What?

LEE. Remember I emptied my bank account for the bike?

ROSE. So?

LEE. The bank has just been closed by the government! It's broke. There's a whole mob of people yelling where's their money! They've got cops and everything! There is no more money in the bank!

ROSE. You're a genius!

LEE. Imagine! – I could have lost my twelve dollars! – Wow!

ROSE. That's wonderful. (*She removes a pearl choker and sits staring at it in her hand.*)

LEE. Don't you love Brooklyn, Ma? We ought to plant some kind of fruit tree in the backyard. Imagine, go out and pick an apple or something? (*Now he sees the pearls. Moved.*) Oh, Ma, really?

ROSE. I hate to; it was Papa's wedding present.

LEE. But what about Papa's business! Can't he? ...

ROSE. He put too much capital in the market, dear – it

made more there than in his business. So now . . . it's not there anymore. (*A thief swiftly appears, and rides the bike Off.*) But we'll be all right. Be careful. Go. You can have a jelly sandwich when you come back. (LEE *stuffs the pearls into his pants as he approaches where the bike was; looks in all directions, his bones chilling. He runs upstage and down, and to left and right and finally comes to a halt, breathless, stark horror on his face. As though sensing trouble,* ROSE *leaves her chair and walks over to him.*) Where's your bike? (*He can't speak.*) They stole your bike? (*He is immobile.*) May he choke on his next meal. (*She embraces him.*) Oh, my darling, my darling, what an awful thing. (*He sobs once, but holds it back. She holds him by the shoulders, facing him, and tries to smile.*) So now you're going to have to walk to the hockshop like everybody else. (*She makes him laugh.*) Come, have your jelly sandwich.

LEE. No, I'd like to see if I can trot there – it'd be good for my track. By the way, I'm almost decided to go to Cornell, I think. Cornell or Brown.

ROSE (*an empty, congratulatory, exclamation*). Oh! – Well, there's still months to decide. (*She puts a hand over her eyes in sorrow. She goes.* ROBERTSON *enters.* LEE *is staring front*).

LEE. I guess that's when I knew there was a system. (*The crowing of a cock. Light transforming to dawn.*)

ROBERTSON. Meaning what, exactly?

LEE. Things that had always seemed fixed and frozen forever were melting, slipping away. One man alone began to seem like a ridiculous idea. (*A swelling crowd of farmers emerges, dressed in mackinaws, pea jackets, big sweaters, checked caps, denim caps; blowing on hands, kicking boots together for warmth.* HENRY TAYLOR *is sitting on the ground to one side.*) What could be a more conservative image? – the Iowa farmer! Yet there they were, turning over milk trucks, dumping thousands of gallons across the highways!

ROBERTSON. That was to create scarcity and raise prices. A perfectly conservative thing to do.

LEE. Huh! – Why did it seem so revolutionary?

ROBERTSON. Oh! – That was that other little number they started to do. (*He moves aside to observe as* BREWSTER *steps forward.*)

BREWSTER (*calling front to the crowd*). Just sit tight, fellas, be startin' in a few minutes.

FARMER 1. Boy, this is one hell of an August. Looks like snow up there.

FARMER 2 (*laughs*). Even the weather ain't workin'. (*Low laughter in the crowd.*)

BREWSTER (*heading over to* HENRY TAYLOR). You be catchin' cold, sitting on the ground like that, won't you, Henry?

HENRY. Tired out. Never slept a wink all night. Not a wink. (MRS TAYLOR *appears in overcoat, carrying a big coffee pot, accompanied by* HARRIET, *the fifteen-year-old daughter, who has a coffee mug hanging from each of her fingers.*)

MRS TAYLOR. You'll have to share the cups, but it's something hot anyway.

BREWSTER. Oh, that smells good, lemme take that, Mrs Taylor. (*She gives the coffee pot to* BREWSTER *and comes over to* HENRY, *her husband.* HARRIET *hands out the cups.*)

MRS TAYLOR (*sotto voce, irritated and ashamed*). You can't be sitting on the ground like that, now come on! (*She starts him to his feet; he stands.*) It's a auction – anybody's got a right to come to a auction.

HENRY. There must be a thousand men along the road – they never told me they'd bring a thousand men!

MRS TAYLOR. Well, I suppose that's the way they do it.

HENRY. They got guns in those trucks!

MRS TAYLOR (*frightened herself*). Well it's too late to stop 'em now. So might as well go around and talk to people that come to help you.

CHARLEY (*Rushes on*). Brewster! Where's Brewster!

BREWSTER (*steps forward from the crowd*). What's up, Charley?

CHARLEY (*points Off*). Judge Bradley! He's gettin' out of the car with the auctioneer! (*Silence. All look to* BREWSTER.)

BREWSTER. Well ... I don't see what that changes. (*Turning to all.*) I guess we're gonna do what we come here to do. That right? (*The crowd quietly agrees – 'Right,' 'Stick to it, Larry,' 'No use quittin' now,' etc. Enter* JUDGE BRADLEY, *sixty, and* MR FRANK HOWARD, *the auctioneer. Silence spreads.*)

JUDGE BRADLEY. Good morning, gentlemen. (*Looks about. There is no reply.*) I want to say a few words to you before Mr Howard starts the auction. (*He walks up on to a raised platform.*) I have decided to come here personally this morning in order to emphasise the gravity of the situation that has developed in the state. We are on the verge of anarchy in Iowa, and that is not going to help anybody. Now you are all property owners, so you –

BREWSTER. Used to be, Judge, used to be!

JUDGE BRADLEY. Brewster, I will not waste words; there are forty armed deputies out there. (*Slight pause.*) I would like to make only one point clear – I have levied a deficiency judgment on this farm. Mr Taylor has failed to pay what he owes on his equipment, and some of his cattle. A contract is sacred. The National Bank has the right to collect on its loans. Now then, Mr

Howard will begin the auction. But he has discretionary power to decline any unreasonable bid. I ask you again, obey the law. Once law and order go down, no man is safe. Mr Howard?

MR HOWARD (*with a clipboard in hand, climbs on to the platform*). Well, now, let's see. We have here one John Deere tractor and combine, three years old, beautiful condition. (*Three bidders enter together – and the crowd turns to look hostilely at them as they come to a halt.*) I ask for bids on the tractor and com –

BREWSTER. Ten cents!

MR HOWARD. I have ten cents. (*His finger raised, he points from man to man in the crowd.*) I have ten cents, I have ten cents ... (*He is pointing towards the bidders, but they are looking around at the crowd in fear.*)

JUDGE BRADLEY (*calls*). Get over here and protect these men! (CALDWELL, *wearing a deputy's star, and four other deputies enter and edge their way in around the three bidders. The deputies carry shotguns.*)

MR HOWARD. Do I hear five hundred dollars? Do I hear five –

BIDDER I. Five hundred! (*Disciplined and quick,* CHARLEY *rushes up – and the farmers grab the deputies and disarm them; a shotgun goes off harmlessly.* BREWSTER *is instantly on to the platform where he pins the* JUDGE'S *arms and another man lowers a noose around his neck.*)

JUDGE BRADLEY. Brewster – Great God, what are you doing!

BREWSTER (*calling out towards other deputies off.*) You come any closer and we're gonna string him up! You all get back on that road or we string up the Judge! So help me Christ he goes up if any one of you deputies interferes with this action! Now let me just clear up one thing for you, Judge Bradley ...

HENRY. Let him go, Brewster – I don't care anymore, let them take it!

BREWSTER. Just sit tight, Henry, nobody's takin' anything. That is all over, Judge. Mr Howard, just to save time, why don't you take a bid on the whole place? Do that, please?

MR HOWARD (*turns to the crowd, his voice shaking*). I . . . I'll hear bids on . . . everything. Tractor and combine, pair of mules and wagon, twenty-six cows, eight heifers, assorted tools . . . and so forth. Do I hear . . .

BREWSTER. One dollar.

MR HOWARD (*rapidly*). I hear one dollar. One dollar, one dollar? . . . (*Looks about.*) Sold for one dollar.

BREWSTER (*handing him a dollar*). Now will you just sign that receipt please? (MR HOWARD *scribbles, hands him a receipt.* BREWSTER *leaps off platform, goes over to* HENRY TAYLOR, *and hands him the receipt.*) Henry? Whyn't you go along now and get to milkin'. Let's go, boys. (*He stands, with a wave, and the crowd quickly follows him out.* BRADLEY *removes the noose and comes down off the platform, goes over to* HENRY TAYLOR, *who is staring down at the receipt.*)

JUDGE BRADLEY. Henry Taylor? You are nothing but a thief! (TAYLOR *cringes under the accusation. The* JUDGE *points to the receipt.*) That is a crime against every law of God and man! And this isn't the end of it either! (*He turns and stalks out.*)

HARRIET. Should we milk 'em, Papa?

MRS TAYLOR. Of course we milk 'em – they're ours. (*But she needs* TAYLOR's *compliance.*) Henry?

HENRY (*staring at the receipt*). It's like I stole my own place. (*Near tears, humiliated,* TAYLOR *moves into darkness with his wife. The farmers disperse.* MOE *enters.*)

MOE. When you say three hundred dollars tuition . . .
Lee! (LEE *enters from opposite side of stage with college
catalogues.*)

LEE. . . . That's for Columbia. Some of these others are
cheaper.

MOE. But that's for the four years.

LEE. Well, no, that's one year.

MOE. Ah. (*He lies back in chair, closes eyes.* LEE *flips a
page of a catalogue.*)

LEE. Minnesota here is a hundred and fifty, for instance.
And Ohio State is about the same, I think. (*Turns to*
MOE, *awaits reaction.*) Pa? (MOE *is asleep.* LEE *closes
catalogue and looks front.*) He always got drowsy when
the news got bad. (*Moves downstage.*) And the mystery
of the marked house began. You'd see the stranger
coming down the street – poor and ragged – and he'd
go past house after house, but at our driveway he'd
make a nice self-assured turn right up to the back porch
and ask for something to eat. Why us? (TAYLOR *appears at one side of the stage. In mackinaw, farm shoes,
peaked hunter's cap, a creased paper bag under his arm.
Looking front he seems gaunt, out of his element; now he
rings doorbell. Nothing happens. He then summons cour-
age and rings again.* LEE *goes to door.*) Yes?

HENRY (*shyly – still an amateur at the routine*). Ah . . . sorry
to be botherin' you on a Sunday and all. (ROSE *enters,
wearing house-dress and apron, wiping hands on a towel.*)

ROSE. Who is that, dear? (*She comes to the door.*)

LEE. This is my mother.

HENRY. How de do, ma'am, my name is Taylor and I'm
just passing by, wondering if you folks have any work
around the place . . .

MOE (*springs up*). Hey! The bell rang! (*Sees the conclave.*)
Oh . . .

ROSE (*ironically*). Another one looking for work!

HENRY. I could paint the place, or fix the roof, electrical, plumbing, masonry, gardening . . . I always had my own farm and we do all that, don't you know. I'd work cheap . . .

ROSE. Well we don't need any kind of . . .

MOE. Where you from?

HENRY. State of Iowa.

LEE ( – *it's the moon*). *Iowa!*

HENRY. I wouldn't charge hardly any more than if I could have my meals, don't you know. 'Course you'd have to provide materials.

MOE (*he is beginning to locate* TAYLOR *in space*). Whereabouts in Iowa?

ROSE. My sister's husband comes from Cleveland.

MOE. No – no, Cleveland is nowhere near. (*To* HENRY.) Whereabouts?

HENRY. You know Styles?

MOE. I only know the stores in the big towns.

HENRY (*a grateful chuckle*). Well! I never expected to meet a . . . (*He gets suddenly dizzy and breaks off and reaches for some support.* LEE *holds his arm and he goes down like an elevator and sits there.*)

ROSE. What's the matter!

MOE. Mister?

LEE. I'll get water! (*He rushes out.*)

ROSE. Is it your heart?

HENRY. 'Scuse me . . . I'm awful sorry . . . (*He gets on hands and knees as* LEE *enters with glass of water and hands it to him. He drinks half of it, returns glass.*) Thank you, sonny.

ROSE (*asking* MOE'S *opinion-agreement – she indicates within*). He better sit down.

MOE. You want to sit down? (HENRY *looks at him help-*

*lessly.*) Come in, sit down. (LEE *and* MOE *help* HENRY *to a chair and he sits.*)

ROSE (*bends over to look into his face*). You got some kind of heart?

HENRY (*embarrassed, and afraid for himself now*). Would you be able to give me something to eat? (*The three stare at him; he looks up at their shocked astonishment and weeps.*)

ROSE. You're *hungry*?

HENRY. Yes, ma'am. (*She looks at* MOE *whether to believe this.*)

MOE (*urgently*). Better get him something.

ROSE (*hurrying out immediately*). Oh my God in heaven!

MOE (*with a suspicious, even accusatory edge*). What're you doing, just going around? . . .

HENRY. Well, no, I come East when I lost the farm . . . they was supposed to be hiring in New Jersey, pickers for the celery? But I only got two days . . . I been to the Salvation Army four, five times, but they only give me a bun and a cup of coffee yesterday . . .

LEE. You haven't eaten since yesterday?

HENRY. . . . Well, I generally don't need too much . . . (ROSE *enters with tray, bowl of soup, and bread.*)

ROSE. I was just making it so I didn't put in the potatoes yet . . .

HENRY. Oh, beets?

ROSE. That's what you call borscht.

HENRY (*obediently*). Yes, ma'am. (*He wastes no time, spoons it up. They all watch him, their first hungry man.*)

MOE (*sceptically*). How do you come to lose a farm?

HENRY. I suppose you read about the Farmers' Uprisin' in the state couple months ago?

LEE. I did.

MOE (*to* LEE). What uprising?

LEE. They nearly lynched a judge for auctioning off their farms. (*To* HENRY, *impressed*.) Were you in *that*?

HENRY. Well, it's all over now, but I don't believe they'll be auctioning any more farms for a while, though. Been just terrible out there.

ROSE (*shaking her head*). And I thought they were all Republicans in Iowa.

HENRY. Well, I guess they all are.

LEE. Is that what they mean by radical, though?

HENRY. Well . . . it's like they say – people in Iowa are practical. They'll even go radical if it seems like it's practical. But as soon as it stops being practical they stop being radical.

MOE. Well, you probably all learned your lesson now.

LEE. Why! – He was taking their homes away, that judge!

MOE. So you go in a court and lynch him?

LEE. But . . . but it's all *wrong*, Pa!

ROSE. Shh! – Don't argue . . .

LEE (*to her*). But *you* think it's wrong, don't you? – Suppose they came and threw us out of *this* house?

ROSE. I refuse to think about it. (*To* HENRY.) So where do you sleep?

MOE (*instantly*). Excuse me. We are not interested in where you sleep, Mister . . . What's your name?

HENRY. Taylor. I'd be satisfied with just my meals if I could live in the basement . . .

MOE (*to* HENRY, *but half-addressing* ROSE). There is no room for another human being in this house, y'understand? – including the basement. (*He takes out two or three bills.*)

HENRY. I wasn't asking for charity . . .

MOE. I'm going to loan you a dollar and I hope you're going to start a whole new life. Here . . . (*Hands* HENRY *the bill, escorting him to the door.*) And pay me back but

don't rush. (*Holds out his hand.*) Glad to have met you,
and good luck.

HENRY. Thanks for the soup, Mrs . . .

ROSE. Our name is Baum. You have children?

HENRY. One's fifteen, one's nine. (*He thoughtfully folds
the dollar bill.* GRANDPA *enters eating a plum.*)

ROSE. Take care of yourself and write a letter to your
wife.

HENRY. Yes, I will. (*To* MOE.) Good-bye, sir . . .

MOE (*grinning, tipping his finger at him*). Stay away from
rope.

HENRY. Oh yeah, I will . . . (*He goes.*)

LEE (*goes out on the periphery and calls to him as he walks
away*). Good-bye, Mr Taylor!

HENRY (*turns back, waves*). Bye, sonny! (*He leaves.* LEE
*stares after him absorbing it.*)

GRANDPA. Who was that?

MOE. He's a farmer from Iowa. He tried to lynch a judge
so she wanted him to live in the cellar.

GRANDPA. What is a farmer doing here?

ROSE. He went broke, he lost everything.

GRANDPA. Oh. Well, he should borrow.

MOE (*snaps his fingers – to* LEE). I'll run down the street
and tell him! He got me hungry. (*To* ROSE.) I'm going
down the corner and get a chocolate soda . . . What do
you say, Lee?

LEE. I don't feel like it.

MOE. Don't be sad. Life is tough, what're you going to
do? Sometimes it's not as tough as other times, that's
all. But it's always tough. Come, have a soda.

LEE. Not now, Pa, thanks. (*He turns away.*)

MOE (*straightens, silently refusing blame*). Be back right
away. (*He strolls away across the stage, softly, tone-
lessly whistling. He goes.* GRANDPA, *chewing, the*

*plum pit in his hand, looks around for a place to put
it.* ROSE *sees the inevitable and holds out her
hand . . .)*

ROSE (*disgusted*). Oh, give it to me. (GRANDPA *drops it
into her palm and she goes out with it and the soup
plate.*)

LEE (*still trying to digest it*). That man was starving,
Grandpa.

GRANDPA. No – no, he was hungry but not starving.

LEE. He was, he almost fainted.

GRANDPA. No, that's not starving. In Europe they starve,
but here not. Anyway, couple weeks they're going to
figure out what to do and you can forget the whole
thing . . . God makes one person at a time, boy – worry
about yourself. (ROBERTSON *enters.*)

ROBERTSON. How did you react to that advice?

LEE. It was ridiculous – how could you only think of
yourself when fellows with advanced degrees were out
on the block throwing footballs around all day! –
Some-big was wrong! – How'd it seem up where you
were?

ROBERTSON. Well of course the rich are always quicker
to be radicalised. Too much at stake to wait around
waiting for something to happen. So the American
Banking Association promptly asked the new Admini-
stration to nationalise the banks.

LEE. What!!

ROBERTSON. It had all gone out of control – they knew
that. Did you know it?

LEE. All I knew was . . . (*He picks up a catalogue, opens it
idly.*) . . . it was a very strange July. I'd graduated high
school but nobody was mentioning college anymore. It
was like having to . . . invent your life. (ROSE *has
entered, sits reading a book.* LEE *points to catalogue.*) In

Cornell there's no tuition fee at all if you enrol for the bacteriology degree.

ROSE. None *at all*?

LEE. It's what it says. Maybe they're short of bacteriologists.

ROSE. That would be wonderful! Would you like that?

LEE (*stares; sees himself as bacteriologist. Sighs*). I don't know. Bacteriology?

ROSE (*wrinkles her nose*). Must be awful. Is anything else free?

LEE. It's the only one I've seen. – Boy, I wish I'd gotten better marks. I don't know what I was doing in school.

ROSE. You were in love with a baseball bat.

LEE. . . . I might've gotten a scholarship or something.

ROSE. I had a scholarship. But Grandpa couldn't wait to marry me off. (*Shakes her head.*) Two days before graduation the girl who was supposed to recite 'The Ancient Mariner' got a quinsy sore throat, so I had two days to learn 'The Ancient Mariner'.

LEE (*shakes his head*). Wow.

ROSE. And I got up there . . . without a mistake. They were spellbound.

LEE. I could never memorise like that.

ROSE. You've got a cat's head. You're always surprised – every morning the world starts up for the first time.

LEE (*mournfully*). I know. (*Thumbing a catalogue.*) Syracuse has –

ROSE. I've got to finish this before tomorrow. I'm overdue fourteen cents on it.

LEE. What is it?

ROSE. *Coronet* by Manuel Komroff. It's about this royal crown that gets stolen and lost and found again and lost again for generations. It's supposed to be literature, but I don't know, it's very enjoyable. (*She goes back to her book.*)

LEE (*closes all the catalogues, looks at her*). Ma?

ROSE (*still reading*). Hm?

LEE (*gently breaking the ice*). I guess it's too late to apply for this year anyway. Don't you think so?

ROSE (*turns to him*). Well, I guess probably for this year. I imagine so, dear.

LEE. Okay, Ma.

ROSE. I feel so terrible – all those years we were throwing money around, and now when you need it –

LEE (*relieved, now that he knows*). That's okay. I think maybe I'll try looking for a job. But I'm not sure whether to look under 'Help Wanted, Male', or 'Boy Wanted'.

ROSE. Boy. (*Their gazes meet. She sees his apprehension.*) Don't be frightened, darling – you're going to be wonderful! (*She hides her feeling in the book. She goes as the light dims.*)

LEE. (*coming centre, facing front*). Like all the winds had stopped, gone dead. (*Light on* SIDNEY *picking out a tune on a piano.*) So anything that moved at all seemed hopeful. (FANNY, SIDNEY's *mother, enters, stands watching him, arms akimbo.*) And nothing could move like my aunt, Two-Gun Fanny Margolies. (*He goes.*)

FANNY. Sidney? (SIDNEY *sings opening line of 'Brother Can You Spare a Dime'.* FANNY *interrupts.*) Sidney? (SIDNEY *sings second line of song, oblivious.*) Sidney? (*He hears now but sings on.*) I have to talk to you, Sidney. (*He plays soft chords – evasively.*) Stop that for a minute!

SIDNEY (*stops playing*). Ma, look . . . it's only July. If I was still in high school it would still be my summer vacation.

FANNY. And if I was the queen of Rumania I would have free rent. You graduated, Sidney, this is not summer vacation.

SIDNEY. Mama, it's useless to go to employment agencies – there's grown men there – engineers, college graduates. They're willing to take anything. If I could write one hit song like this, just one – we wouldn't have to worry again. Let me have July, just July; see if I can do it. Because that man was serious – he's a good friend of the waiter who works where Bing Crosby's manager eats. He could give him any song I write, and if Crosby just sang it one time . . .

FANNY. I want to talk to you about Doris.

SIDNEY. What Doris?

FANNY. Doris! Doris from downstairs. I've been talking to her mother. – She likes you, Sidney.

SIDNEY. Who?

FANNY. Her mother! Mrs Gross. She's crazy about you.

SIDNEY (*not comprehending*). Oh.

FANNY. She says all Doris does is talk about you.

SIDNEY (*worried*). What is she talking about me for?

FANNY. No, nice things. She likes you.

SIDNEY (*amused, laughs incredulously*). *Doris?* – She's thirteen.

FANNY. She'll be fourteen in December. Now listen to me.

SIDNEY. What, Ma?

FANNY. It's all up to you, Sidney, I want you to make up your own mind. But Papa's never going to get off his back again and after Theresa's wedding we can forget about *her* salary. Mrs Gross says – being she's a widow, y'know? And with her goitre and everything . . .

SIDNEY. What?

FANNY. If you like Doris – only if you like her – and you would agree to get married. – When she's eighteen, about, or seventeen, even – if you would agree to it now, we could have this apartment rent-free. Starting next month.

SIDNEY (*impressed, even astounded*). Forever?

FANNY. Of course. You would be the husband, it would be your house. You'd move downstairs, with that grand piano and the tile shower . . . I even think if you'd agree she'd throw in the three months' back rent that we owe. I wouldn't even be surprised you could take over the bakery.

SIDNEY. The bakery! For God's sake, Mama, I'm a composer!

FANNY. Now listen to me . . . (DORIS *enters, sits at a distance and plays cat's cradle with string.*)

SIDNEY. But how can I be a baker!

FANNY. Sidney, dear, did you ever once look at that girl?

SIDNEY. Why should I look at her!

FANNY (*taking his arm, and turning him towards* DORIS). Because she's a beauty. I wouldn't have mentioned it otherwise. Look. Look at that nose. Look at her hands. You see those beautiful little white hands? You don't find hands like that everywhere.

SIDNEY. But, Ma, listen – if you just leave me alone for July, and if I write one hit song . . . I know I can do it, Mama.

FANNY. Okay. Sidney, we're behind a hundred and eighty dollars. August first we're out on the street. So write a hit, dear. I only hope that four, five years from now you don't accidentally run into Doris Gross somewhere and fall in love with her – after we all died from exposure!

SIDNEY. But Ma, even if I agreed – supposing next year or the year after I meet some other girl and I really like *her* . . .

FANNY. All right, and supposing you marry *that* girl and a year after you meet another girl you like better –

what are you going to do, get married every year? . . .
But I only wanted you to know the situation. I'll close
the door, everything'll be quiet. Write a big hit, Sidney.
(*She goes out. Alone, he avoids looking in* DORIS'*s direction, goes in conflict to the piano, and touches the keys
without sitting down. A pause. He turns towards* DORIS.
*Then walks across to her. She continues playing cat's
cradle. Slowly, he sits on his heels.*)

SIDNEY. Gee . . . you're really terrific at that, Doris.
(DORIS *rises to him; they look – for different reasons –
rather desperately at one another. He starts to walk, she
catches up, and he slips his hand around hers as they go.
Light on* MOE *and* ROSE; *she is in a housecoat and slippers,
he in a business suit and hat. He is just giving her a peck.*)

ROSE. Good-bye, darling; this is going to be a good day –
I know it!

MOE (*not too much conviction*). I think you're right. G'bye.
(*He walks. Gradually comes to a halt. Much uncertainty
and tension as he glances back towards his house and then
looks down to think.* LEE *enters and* ROSE *gives him a fare-
well kiss. He wears a mackinaw and has a lunch bag and
a book under his arm.*)

ROSE (*indicating his lunch bag*). Don't squeeze it, I put in
some cookies . . . And listen – it doesn't mean you can
*never* go to college.

LEE. Oh, I don't mind, Ma. – Anyway, I like it around
machines. I'm lucky I got the job!

ROSE. All the years we had so much and now when you
need it –

LEE (*cutting her off*). See ya! (*He leaves her; she goes; he
walks and is startled by* MOE *standing there.*) I thought
you left a long time ago!

MOE. I'll walk you a way. (*Doesn't bother explaining,
simply walks beside* LEE, *but at a much slower pace than*

LEE *had before.* LEE *feels his unusual tension but can only glance over at him with growing apprehension and puzzlement. Finally.*) . . . Good job?

LEE. It's okay. I couldn't believe they picked me!

MOE (*nods*). Good. (*They walk again in silence, weaving all over the stage, the tension growing as* LEE *keeps glancing at* MOE, *who continuously stares down and ahead as they proceed. Now at last* MOE *halts and takes a deep breath.*) How much money've you got, Lee?

LEE (*completely taken aback*). . . . Money have I got?

MOE (*indicating* LEE's *pockets*). I mean right now.

LEE. Oh! Well about – (*He takes out change.*) – thirty-five cents. I'm okay.

MOE. . . . Could I have a quarter? – So I can get downtown.

LEE (*an instant; astonished; then*). Oh sure, Pa! (*He quickly searches in his pockets.*)

MOE. You got your lunch – I'll need a hot dog later. (LEE *hands him a quarter.*)

LEE. It's okay. I have a dollar in my drawer . . . Should I? . . . (*Starts to go back.*)

MOE. No, don't go back. (*Proceeds to walk again.*) Don't, ah . . . mention it, heh?

LEE. Oh no!

MOE (*who has come to a halt*). She worries.

LEE. I know. (*To the audience, as* MOE *goes.*) We got on the subway together and it was hard to look at one another. So pretended that nothing had happened. But something had. – It was like I'd started to support my *father*! And why that should have made me feel so happy, I don't know, but it did! And to cheer him up I began to talk and before I knew it I was inventing a fantastic future! (*Laughs.*) I said I'd be going to college in no more than a year, at most, two; and that I'd straighten out my mind and become an A student; and then I'd not only get a job on a newspaper, but I'd have my own column, no less! – By the time we got to Forty-Second Street the Depression was practically over! (*Laughs. Music.*) And in a funny way, it *was* – (*Touches his breast.*) – in here . . . even though I knew we had a long bad time ahead of us. – And so, like most people, I waited with that crazy kind of expectation that comes when there is no hope, waited for the dream to come back from wherever it had gone to hide. (*He turns and walks, putting on his cap, and as he passes out of his light,* ROBERTSON *appears – once again an old grey-haired man with a serious grin.*)

ROBERTSON. By my twenty-fourth birthday I had a seven-figure income; I considered retiring at twenty-eight. I've been a little of everything – war correspondent, ad-man, engineer – we built a section of the Sixth Avenue subway, in fact. – I've worked in many countries, but I guess the most shocking thing I ever saw was from the window of my Riverside Drive apartment. It was like Calcutta, thousands of people living in cardboard boxes, tin shanties along the Hudson River right below the Drive – at night their campfires flickered right down the length of Manhattan Island, like an army encampment. Some nights I'd go down and walk among them; remarkable, the humour they still had, and of course people still blamed themselves rather than the government. But there's never been a society that hasn't had a clock running on it and you couldn't help wondering – how long? How long would they stand for this? There were nights you could almost hear it in the air . . . (*He clucks his tongue like a clock, glaring out, continuing until . . .*)

*Curtain.*

## Act Two

ROSE *is discovered walking up and down in agitation near the piano. She halts, stares, speaks.*

ROSE. But this piano is not leaving this house. Jewellery, yes, but nobody hocks this dear, darling piano. (*Plays, sings opening line of 'I Can't Give You Anything but Love, Baby'.*) The crazy ideas people get. Mr Warsaw on our block, to make a little money he started a race-track in his kitchen, with cockroaches. Keeps them in matchboxes with their names written on – 'Alvin', 'Murray', 'Irving' . . . They bet nickels, dimes. (*Picks up sheet music.*) Oh, what a show, that 'Funny Face'. (*Sings opening lines of 'He Loves and She Loves'.*) The years go by you and don't get to see a show and Brooklyn drifts further and further into the Atlantic; Manhattan becomes a foreign country and a year can go by without ever going there. (*Sings more of 'He Loves and She Loves'.*) Wherever you look there's a contest; Kellogg's, Post Toasties win five thousand, win ten thousand. Maybe I ought to try but the winners are always in Indiana, somehow. I only pray to God our health holds up because one inlay and there go the new hinges for the refrigerator. Sing! (*She sings opening of 'Do-Do-Do What You Done-Done-Done Before'.*) I must go to the library – I must start taking out some good books again; I must stop getting so stupid. I don't see anything, I don't hear anything except money, money, money . . . (*Plays Schumann. Then stops in frus-*

*tration and walks into darkness.* LEE *emerges in the spot-light with three fellow students wearing graduation caps and gowns. He is in a sweater. They are a quartet, singing, 'Down by the Old Mill Stream'. He steps forward as the others hum their harmony.* ROBERTSON *emerges, observes.*)

LEE. The very best place to be was school. Two pairs of socks, a shirt, a good shirt, and a mackinaw; part-time job in the library maybe – you could live like a king and practically never see cash.

ROBERTSON. Could that be why it held together as well as it did? – People saw how little they really needed, and maybe that gave them a new happiness.

LEE. You could keep the razor blade sharp for six months by rubbing it around in a drinking glass – you got to know that razor blade.

ROBERTSON. And naturally there were some tremendous new opportunities – banks foreclosing on some first-class properties that you could pick up for a song.

LEE (*rejoins quartet to finish song*). Boy, I hope next year's batch of guys can sing. (*He hugs his old friend* JOEY.) Is it possible, Joe!

JOE. What?

LEE. You're a dentist! (ROBERTSON *goes, smiling.*)

RALPH (*extending his hand*). Well, it was nice knowing you, Lee.

LEE (*shaking hands*). You decide what to do?

RALPH. There's supposed to be a small aircraft plant still working in Louisville . . .

LEE. Too bad you picked propellers for a specialty.

RALPH. Oh, they'll make aeroplanes again; if there's ever a war, you'll see.

LEE. How could there be another war?

JOE. Long as there's capitalism, baby.

RALPH. There'll always be war, y'know, according to the Bible. But if not, I'll probably go into the ministry.

LEE. I never knew you were religious.

RALPH. I'm sort of religious. They pay pretty good, you know, and you get your house and a clothing allowance . . .

JOE (*comes over, hand extended*). Don't forget to read Karl Marx, Lee. And if you're ever in the neighbourhood with a toothache look me up. I'll keep an eye out for your by-line.

LEE. Oh, I don't expect a newspaper job – papers are closing all over the place. Drop me a card if you open an office.

JOE. It'll probably be in my girl's father's basement. He promised to dig the floor out deeper so I can stand up . . .

LEE. What about equipment?

JOE. I figure two, three years I'll be able to open, if I can make a down payment on a used drill. Come by, I'll put back those teeth Ohio State knocked out.

LEE. I sure will! So long, Rudy!

RUDY. Oh, you might still be seeing me around next semester.

JOE. You staying on campus?

RUDY. I might for the sake of my root canals. There's a group of physicists taking over one of those abandoned houses on Lawrence Avenue – it's a little dark with all the windows boarded up, but it's rent-free, and if I just take one university course I'm still entitled to the Health Service – could get my canals finished.

LEE. You mean there's a course in the Lit School you haven't taken?

RUDY. Yeah, I just found out about it. 'Roman Band Instruments.'

JOE (*laughs*). You're kiddin'!

RUDY. No, in the Classics Department. 'Roman Band Instruments.' (*Pulls his cheek back.*) See, I've still got three big ones to go on this side. (*Laughter.*) Well, if you really face it, where am I running? Chicago's loaded with anthropologists. Here, the university's like my mother – I've got free rent, wash dishes for my meals, get my teeth fixed, and God knows, I might pick up the paper one morning and there's an ad: 'Help Wanted: Handsome young college graduate, good teeth, must be thoroughly acquainted with Roman band instruments'! (*Laughter.*)

RALPH. Hey, come on, we'll be late! I hope things are better by the time you get out, Lee. I'll keep looking for your by-line anyway.

LEE. No, I doubt it; but I might angle a job on a Mississippi paddleboat.

RUDY. They still run those?

LEE. Yeah, there's a few. I'd like to retrace Mark Twain's voyages.

RUDY. Well, if you run into Huckleberry Finn –

LEE. I'll give him your regards. (*Laughing,* RALPH *and* RUDY *start out.*)

RALPH. Beat Ohio State, kid!

JOE (*alone with* LEE *he gives him a clenched-fist salute*). So long, Lee.

LEE (*returning the salute*). So long, Joe! (*They are gone. Alone,* LEE *mimes pulling on a boat whistle. And quietly, to himself . . .*) Tooot! Tooooot! (*Blackout. Music. Lights emblazon the map at rear, the full breadth of the country appearing. Light on* LEE. *He is greasy, bare to the waist, wiping sweat off his face.*) Dear Mom and Pa. It's not really a job because they don't pay me, but they let me eat in the galley and I sleep on deck. The Mississippi is so beautiful, but sometimes it's frightening. Yesterday we stopped at a little town where they were handing out beans and meat to the hungry. The meat was full of maggots, you could see them wriggling out when the butcher cut into it. Suddenly a man with a gun pointed it at the butcher and forced him to give out the good meat which the government had paid him for, but which he kept for his paying customers. I keep trying to imagine how Mark Twain would deal with a scene like that. I don't understand how people are managing to live; a great many banks are boarded up. And there hasn't been rain for months; even the sky dried out. Every town is full of men sitting on the sidewalks with their backs against the storefronts. Just looking at you, or asleep. It's like a magic spell. I keep trying to find the holes in Marxism but I can't. I just read an article where the salaries of twelve executives in the tobacco business were more than thirty thousand tobacco farmers made. That's why this happened – the workers never made enough to buy back what they produced. The boom of the twenties was a gigantic fake. The rich have simply looted the people. And all President Hoover can say is to have confidence! I've passed fields of corn rotting on the stalks unsold, and sheriffs guarding them while on the roads people fall down from hunger. – There is going to be a revolution, Mama . . . (LEE *goes. Light on* ROSE *entering; she is reading from a letter.*)

ROSE. '. . . You can smell it in the air. I am going to try to find some way to help it happen.' But how is he ever going to become a sportswriter if he's a Communist? (*Three men enter, lower the top of the piano;* ROSE *hesitates, then gathers up her music and softly closes the keyboard cover. The men move the piano and bench out. She stands motionless, her face tired. She walks into darkness. Light up on* JOE. *He carries a large basket of flowers.*)

JOE (*facing audience*). Dear Lee. Sounds great in Mississippi, almost as good as here. I'm writing this in a whorehouse. I come here to get my sanity back. Such as it is. I decided to give myself one more year. After that I'll be too nervous to pick up an instrument. I may be too nervous now, this is my fear. I hope I'm wrong, but I'm thinking that the more trouble people have the less they question things. They're constantly talking to themselves on the IRT platform; they get so involved they even miss trains. Insanity is taking over. It's amazing how many Americans come up behind me and try to feel my ass. Yesterday, apropos of nothing, a small hunchback starts yelling at me, 'You will not find one word about democracy in the Constitution! This is a Christian republic!' Nobody laughed. The Nazi swastika is blooming all over the toopthpaste ads. I keep my nose in the flower basket but the subway smells of fascism. Up on Forty-Ninth Street and Eighth Avenue you can get two very good hot dogs for seven cents. What can that man make on two for seven cents? Suddenly some bright morning I expect to see millions of people pouring out of the buildings and just – I don't know what. Kill each other? Or only the Jews? Or just sit down on the street and cry? (*A bed is pushed on and* ISABEL *enters.* JOE *puts a second pair of pants on.*)

ISABEL. Ain't that uncomfortable, hey? Two pair of pants?

JOE. Gets very cold on the subway platform all day. The wind's like the Gobi Dessert. The only problem is when you run out to pee it takes twice as long.

ISABEL. Sell books too?

JOE. That's for reading. On my way home after work I

trying not to forget the English language. All I hear all day is shit, fuck, and piss.

ISABEL (*turning over the book*). It's about families?

JOE. Not exactly. That's by Engels: *The Origins of the Family and the State.*

ISABEL (*heavily impressed, turns a page*). Huh!

JOE (*a sudden thought*). Hey, why don't try to read it? I'd really like your reaction. You see, it's Marxism – says that all our relationships are basically ruled by money.

ISABEL (*nodding – as she well knows*). Oh, right. Yeah.

JOE. . . . No, I didn't mean exactly that way. (*Changes his mind.*) Although, maybe –

ISABEL. It's a whole *book* about that?

JOE. Well, he's trying to change it, you see. With socialism, the girls would all have jobs so they wouldn't have to do this.

ISABEL. But what would the guys do, though?

JOE (*only slightly flustered*). Well . . . they would just have to, ah . . . For instance, if I had money to open my office, I would probably get married very soon.

ISABEL. But I get married guys. (*Brightly.*) And I got two dentists you brought me . . . Bernie and Allan? . . . and they've got offices.

JOE (*troubled*). You don't understand. He shows that underneath our ideals and so on, it's all economies between people. And it shouldn't be.

ISABEL. You mean it should be like . . . love?

JOE (*not exactly, but . . .*). Ah . . . yeah, well, in a way.

ISABEL. Oh! Well, that's nice hey. (*Opening book again.*) I'd like to read this.

JOE. But don't expect a love story; it's basically theoretical anthropology.

ISABEL (*alarmed*). Oh. Well, I probably wouldn't have time. (*Embarrassed, hands him the book.*) But, hey, I meant to tell you – I know a very nice shark, maybe he could lend you for a drill.

JOE. I borrowed too much already. Here, take a carnation.

ISABEL. Oh – thanks, hey – But maybe keep it and sell it.

JOE. No, go ahead. I like the illusion. Here's your buck. (*Gives her a bill, puts on wool cap.*) Maybe next week, huh?

ISABEL. But couldn't you come a little later, hey? I'm still tired so early in the morning.

JOE. I gotta catch the office girls going to work – they like a flower for the desk. And I like you early; you look fresh, gives me an illusion. – Bernie finish the inlay?

ISABEL (*opening her mouth*). Yeah, he polished yesterday.

JOE (*looking in*). Bernie's good. I told you, we were in the same class. Say I said hello if you see him again.

ISABEL. He said he might come after five, said to give you his best.

JOE. Yeah, give him my best, too.

ISABEL. Till you I never had so many dentists. (ROBERTSON *appears.*)

ROBERTSON. I catch myself feeling smug about the tremendous number of extremist crusades that came roaring down the runway, but never took off. Furious, cruel-talking haters of labour, Jews and blacks and foreigners. Sometimes the political air could stink with hate. And worst of all, after two years or so, you knew that no one really had a solution to this crisis . . . none at all; and it bit closer and closer to the bone. (*Light rises on* LEE. *In dungarees, sitting at a counter eating a slice of watermelon.* ISAAC, *the black proprietor, is wiping the counter which he has just pushed on.*)

ISAAC. You been workin' the river long? I ain't seen you before, have I?

LEE. No, this is my first trip down the river, I'm from New York City. – I'm just kind of looking around the country, talking to people.

ISAAC. What you lookin' around *for*?

LEE. Nothing – just trying to figure out what's happening. Ever hear of Mark Twain?

ISAAC. He from around here?

LEE. Well, long time ago, ya. He was a story writer.

ISAAC. Uh, huh. I ain't seen him around here. You ask at the post office?

LEE. No, but I might. I'm kind of surprised you can get fifteen cents a slice down here these days.

ISAAC. Ohhh – white folks *loves* watermelon. Things bad as this up North?

LEE. Probably not quite. – I sure wouldn't want to be one of you people down here . . . 'specially with this Depression.

ISAAC. Mister, if I was to tell you the God's honest truth, the main thing about the Depression is that it finally hit the white people. 'Cause us folks never had nothin' else. (*Sees offstage.*) Well now – here come the big man.

LEE. He trouble?

ISAAC. He's anything he wants to be, mister – he the sheriff. (SHERIFF *enters – holstered gun, boots, badge, broad-brimmed hat, and carrying something wrapped under his arm. He stares silently at* LEE.)

LEE (*nervous half-apology*). I'm off the boat. (*Indicates offstage.*)

SHERIFF. You don't bother me, boy – relax. (*He sits at counter and sets his package down and turns with gravity to* ISAAC. LEE *makes himself unobtrusive and observes in silence.*) Isaac?

ISAAC. Yes sir. (*After a moment . . .*)

SHERIFF. . . . Sit down.

ISAAC. Yes, sir. (*He sits on another stool; he is intensely curious about the* SHERIFF'S *calling on him but not frightened. Since the* SHERIFF *seems to be having trouble starting the conversation:*) Looks like rain.

SHERIFF (*preoccupied*). Mm. – Hard to know.

ISAAC. Yeah . . . always is in Louisiana. – Anything I can do for you, Sheriff?

SHERIFF. Read the papers today?

ISAAC. I couldn't read my name if an air-o-plane wrote it in the sky, Sheriff, you know that.

SHERIFF. My second cousin Allan? The state senator?

ISAAC. Uh huh?

SHERIFF. The governor just appointed him. He's gonna help run the state police.

ISAAC. Uh huh?

SHERIFF. He's comin' down to dinner Friday night over to my house. Bringin' his wife and two daughters. I'm gonna try to talk to Allan about a job on the state police. They still paying the *state* police, see.

ISAAC. Uh huh. Well that be nice, won't it.

SHERIFF. Isaac, I like you to cook me up some of that magical fried chicken around six o'clock, Friday night. Okay? I'll pick it up.

ISAAC (*noncommittal*). Mm.

SHERIFF. That'd be for . . . let's see . . . (*Counts on his fingers.*) . . . eight people. My brother and his wife comin' over too, 'cause I aim to give Allan a little spread there, get him talkin' real good, y'know?

ISAAC. Mm. (*An embarrassed pause.*)

SHERIFF. What's that gonna cost me for eight people, Isaac?

ISAAC (*at once*). Ten dollars.

SHERIFF. Ten.

ISAAC (*with a little commiseration*). That's right, Sheriff.

SHERIFF (*slight pause. Starts to unwrap radio*). Want to show you something here, Isaac. My radio, see?

ISAAC. Uh huh. (*Runs his hand over it.*) Play?

SHERIFF. Sure! Plays real good. I give twenty-nine ninety-five for that two years ago.

ISAAC (*looks in the back of it*). I plug it in?

SHERIFF. Go right ahead, sure. You sure painted this place up real nice. Like a real restaurant. You oughta thank the Lord, Isaac.

ISAAC (*takes out the wire and plugs it in as . . .*). I sure do. The Lord and fried chicken!

SHERIFF. You know the county ain't paid nobody at all in three months now . . .

ISAAC. Yeah, I know. Where you switch it on?

SHERIFF. Just turn the knob. There you are. (*Turns it on.*) They're still payin' the *state* police, see. And I figure if I can get Allan to put me on – (*Radio music. It is very dim.*)

ISAAC. Cain't hardly hear it.

SHERIFF (*angrily*). Hell, Isaac, gotta get the aerial out! (*Untangling a wire at the back of the set*). You give me eight fried chicken dinners and I let you hold this for collateral, okay? Here we go now. (SHERIFF *backs aways stretching out the aerial wire, and* ROOSEVELT'S *voice suddenly comes on strong.* SHERIFF *holds still, the wire held high.* LEE *is absorbed.*)

ROOSEVELT. Clouds of suspicion, tides of ill-will and intolerance gather darkly in many places. In our own land we enjoy, indeed, a fullness of life . . .

SHERIFF. And nice fat chickens, hear? Don't give me any little old scruffy chickens.

ISAAC (*of* ROOSEVELT). Who's that talkin'?

ROOSEVELT. . . . greater than that of most nations. But the rush of modern civilisation itself has raised for us new difficulties, . . .

SHERIFF. Sounds like somebody up North.

ISAAC. Hush! (*To* LEE.) Hey, that's Roosevelt, ain't it?!

LEE. Yes.

ISAAC. Sure! – That's the President!

SHERIFF. How about it, we got a deal? (ISAAC *has his head close to the radio, absorbed.* LEE *comes closer, bends over to listen.*)

ROOSEVELT. . . . new problems which must be solved if we are to preserve to the United States the political and economic freedom for which Washington and Jefferson planned and fought. We seek not merely to make government a mechanical implement, but to give it the vibrant personal character that is the embodiment of human charity. We are poor indeed if this nation cannot afford to lift from every recess of American life the dark fear of the unemployed that they are not needed in the world. We cannot afford to accumulate a deficit in the books of human fortitude. (*With even the* SHERIFF *caught in the speech, its volume slowly fades . . . light starts to go down as* ISAAC *listens, and the* SHERIFF *still holds the wire. During the above,* LEE *has moved from* ISAAC *and* SHERIFF *as a crowd moves on, the unemployed who pause before a welfare worker who hands each a numbered slip of paper, and then continue off.* LEE *is anxiously looking around in a vast empty space. Now* MOE *appears and joins him. He is deeply anxious.*)

LEE. Hi, Pop! Glad you could get here.

MOE. One minute, Lee, before we go in there . . .

LEE. Look, Pa, if it's too embarrassing . . .

MOE. You sure you know what you're doing? . . . because I distinctly read in the paper that anybody wants to work can go direct to WPA and they fix you up with a job.

LEE. Originally, yes, but they changed it now. You can only get a WPA job now if you're on relief.

MOE. I don't understand that . . .

LEE. Well, there's sixteen million unemployed. They haven't got jobs for everybody.

MOE. Then what's Roosevelt been talking about?

LEE. He probably thought things would improve, and they didn't, so now you've got to be destitute to be eligible for WPA.

MOE (*pointing towards the line*). So this is not the WPA.

LEE. I told you, Pa, this is the relief office.

MOE. Like . . . welfare.

LEE. Look, if it embarrasses you –

MOE. Listen, if it has to be done it has to be done. Now let me go over it again. – What do I say?

LEE. You refuse to let me live in the house. We don't get along.

MOE. Why can't you live at home?

LEE. If I live at home, I don't need relief. That's the rule.

MOE. Okay. So I can't stand the sight of you.

LEE. Right.

MOE. So you live with your friend in a rooming house.

LEE. Correct.

MOE. . . . They're gonna believe that?

LEE. Why not? I've got some of my clothes over there.

MOE. All this for twenty-two dollars a week?

LEE (*angering*). What am I going to do? Even old-time newspapermen are out of work. – See, if I can get on the WPA Writers Project, at least I'd get experience if a real job comes along. I've explained this a dozen times, Pa, there's nothing complicated.

MOE (*unsatisfied*). I'm just trying to get used to it. All

right. Let's go. (*They embrace. Then:*) We shouldn't look too friendly, huh?

LEE (*laughs*). That's the idea!

MOE. I don't like you and you can't stand the sight of me.

LEE. That's it! (*Laughs.*)

MOE (*to the air with mock outrage*). So he laughs! (*The crowd of unemployed enters as a row of warehouse-like lamps lowers over the scene and a table and one chair are carried to Centre. RYAN, the social worker, enters with case folders. People stand around as in an impromptu relief office. Black and white. Old and young. MOE looks around.*)

ROBERTSON. I did a lot of walking in those days. The contrasts were so startling. Along the West side of Manhattan you had eight or ten of the world's greatest ocean liners tied up – I recall the S.S. Manhattan, the Berengaria, the United States – most of them would never sail again. But at the same time they were putting up the Empire State Building, highest in the world. But who would ever rent space in it when there were whole streets and avenues of empty stores? It was incredible to me how long it was lasting. I would never, never have believed we could not recover before this. Whole years were passing, a whole generation was withering in the best years of its life . . . (*The light on him goes out.*)

MOE (*continues*). Well! There's some nice-looking people.

LEE. Sure.

RYAN (*the supervisor, at a desk*). Matthew R. Bush! (*A very dignified man of forty-five rises, crosses, and follows RYAN out.*)

MOE. Looks like a butler.

LEE. Probably was.

MOE (*shakes his head mournfully*). Hmm! (*A baby held by* GRACE, *a young woman in the back, cries.* MOE *turns to look, then stares ahead.*) Lee, what'll you do if they give you a pick-and-shovel job?

LEE. I'll take it.

MOE. You'll dig holes in the streets?

LEE. It's no disgrace, Dad.

KAPUSH (*late sixties, Slavonic, moustache, ferocious frustration*). What can you expect from a country that puts a frankfurter on the Supreme Court? Felix the Frankfurter. Look it up.

DUGAN (*from another part of the room*). Get back in the clock, ya cuckoo!

KAPUSH (*turning his body around angrily to face* DUGAN *and jarring a black woman,* IRENE, *sitting next to him*). Who's talkin' to me!

IRENE (*middle-aged black woman*). Hey now, don't mess with me, mister!

DUGAN. Tell him, tell him! (RYAN *rushes in. He is pale, his waistcoat is loaded with pens and pencils, and a sheaf of papers is in his hand. A tired man.*)

RYAN. We gonna have another riot, folks? Is that what we're gonna have? Mr Kapush, I told you three days running now, if you live in Bronx you've got to apply in Bronx.

KAPUSH. It's all right, I'll wait.

RYAN (*as he passes* DUGAN). Leave him alone, will you? He's a little upset in his mind.

DUGAN. He's a fascist. I seen him down Union Square plenty of times. (IRENE *slams her walking stick down on the table.*)

RYAN. Oh, Jesus . . . here we go again.

IRENE. Gettin' on to ten o'clock, Mr Ryan.

RYAN. I've done the best I can, Irene . . .

IRENE. That's what the good lord said when he made the jackass, but he decided to knuckle down and try harder. People been thrown out on the sidewalk, mattresses, pots and pans, and everything else they own. Right on a Hundred and Thirty-Eighth Street. They goin' back in their apartments today or we goin' raise us some real hell.

RYAN. I've got no more appropriations for you till the first of the month and that's it, Irene.

IRENE. Mr Ryan, you ain't talkin' to me, you talkin' to Local Forty-Five of the Workers Alliance, and you know what that mean.

DUGAN (*laughs*). Communist Party.

IRENE. That's right, mister, and they don't mess. So why don't you get on your phone and call Washington. And while you're at it, you can remind Mr Roosevelt that I done swung One Hundred and Thirty-Ninth Street for him in the last election, and if he want it swung again he better get crackin'!

RYAN. Holy Jesus. (*Hurries away, but* LEE *tries to delay him.*)

LEE. I was told to bring my father.

RYAN. What?

LEE. Yesterday. You told me to –

RYAN. Get off my back, will ya? (*He hurries out.*)

DUGAN. This country's gonna end up on the top of the trees throwin' coconuts at each other.

MOE (*quietly to* LEE). I hope I can get out by eleven, I got an appointment with a buyer.

TOLAND (*Daily News open in his hands. He is next to* MOE). Boy, oh boy, looka this – Helen Hayes gonna put on forty pounds to play Victoria Regina.

MOE. Who's that?

TOLAND. Queen of England.

MOE. She was so fat?

TOLAND. Victoria? Horse. I picked up Helen Hayes when I had my cab. Very small girl. And Adolphe Menjou once – he was small, too. I even had Al Smith once, way back before he was governor. He was real small.

MOE. Maybe you had a small cab.

TOLAND. What do you mean? I had a regular Ford.

MOE. You lost it?

TOLAND. What're you gonna do? You can't make it in a cab anymore. The town is walkin'. I paid five hundred dollars, brand-new Ford, including bumpers and a spare. But thank God, at least I got into the housing project. It's nice and reasonable.

MOE. What do you pay?

TOLAND. Nineteen-fifty a month. It sounds like a lot but we got three nice rooms. – Providin' I get a little help here. What's your line?

MOE. I sell on commission right now. I used to have my own business.

TOLAND. Used-ta. Whoever you talk to, 'I used-ta'. If they don't do something, I tell ya, one of these days this used-ta be a country.

KAPUSH (*exploding*). Ignorance, ignorance! People don't know facts. Greatest public library system in the entire world and nobody goes in but Jews.

MOE (*glancing at him*). Ah ha.

LEE. What're you, Iroquois?

DUGAN. He's a fascist. I seen him talking on Union Square.

IRENE. Solidarity, folks, black and white together, that's what we gotta have. Join the Workers Alliance, ten cents a month, and you git yourself some solidarity.

KAPUSH. I challenge anybody to find the word de-mocracy in the Constitution. This is a republic! *Demos* is the Greek word for mob.

DUGAN (*imitating the bird*). *Cuckoo!*

KAPUSH. Come to get my money and the bank is closed up! Four thousand dollars up the flue. Thirteen years in hardware, savin' by the week.

DUGAN. Mental diarrhoea.

KAPUSH. Mobocracy. Gimme, gimme, gimme, all they know.

DUGAN. So what're *you* doing here?

KAPUSH. Roosevelt was sworn in on a Dutch Bible! (*Silence.*) Anybody know that? (*To* IRENE.) Betcha didn't know that, did you?

IRENE. You givin' me a headache, mister . . .

KAPUSH. I got nothin' against coloured. Coloured never took my store away. Here's my bankbook, see that? Bank of the United States. See that? Four-thousand six-hundred and ten dollars and thirty-one cents, right? Who's got that money? Savin' thirteen years, by the week. *Who's got my money?* (*He has got to his feet. His fury has turned the moment silent.* MATTHEW BUSH *enters and sways.* RYAN *enters.*)

RYAN. Arthur Clayton! (CLAYTON *starts towards* RYAN *and indicates* MATTHEW BUSH.)

CLAYTON. I think there's something the matter with – (BUSH *collapses on the floor. For a moment no one moves. Then* IRENE *goes to him, bends over him.*)

IRENE. Hey. Hey, Mister. (LEE *helps him up and sits him in the chair.*)

RYAN (*calling to offstage*). Myrna, call the ambulance! (IRENE *lightly slaps* BUSH's *cheeks.*)

LEE. You all right?

RYAN (*looking around*). Clayton?

CLAYTON. I'm Clayton.

RYAN (CLAYTON's *form in his hand*). You're not eligible for relief; you've got furniture and valuables, don't you?

CLAYTON. But nothing I could realize anything on.

RYAN. Why not? – Is this your address? Gramercy Park South?

CLAYTON (*embarrassed*). That doesn't mean a thing. I haven't really eaten in a few days, actually . . .

RYAN. Where do you get that kind of rent?

CLAYTON. I haven't paid my rent in over eight months . . .

RYAN (*starting away*). Forget it, mister, you got valuables and furniture; you can't –

CLAYTON. I'm very good at figures, I was in brokerage. I thought if I could get anything that required . . . say, statistics . . .

IRENE. This man's starvin', Mr Ryan.

RYAN. What're you, a medical doctor now, Irene? I called the ambulance! Now don't start makin' an issue, will you? (*He returns to his desk.* CLAYTON *stands there, uncertain.*)

IRENE. Grace? You got anything in that bottle?

GRACE (*in a rear rank with a baby in her arms, reaches forward with a baby bottle which has an inch of milk on the bottom*). Ain't much left there . . .

IRENE (*handed the bottle, takes off the nipple*). Okay now, open your mouth, mister. (BUSH *gulps the milk.*) There, look at that, see? Man's starvin'!

MOE (*stands, reaching into his pocket*). Here . . . look . . . for God's sake. (*Takes out change and picks out a dime.*) Why don't you send down, get him a bottle of milk?

IRENE (*calls towards the back*). Lucy –

LUCY (*a young girl, coming forward*). Here I am, Irene.

IRENE. Go down the corner, bring a bottle of milk. (MOE *gives* LUCY *the dime and she hurries out.*) And a couple of straws, honey! You in bad shape, Mister – why'd you wait so long to get on relief?

BUSH. Well. I just don't like the idea, you know.

IRENE. Yeah, I know – you're a real bourgeois. Let me tell you something –

BUSH. I'm a chemist.

IRENE. I believe it, too – you so educated you sooner die than say brother. Now lemme tell you people. (*She is addressing the crowd.*) Time has come to say brother. My husband pass away and leave me with three small children. No money, no work – I's about ready to stick my head in the cookin' stove. Then the city marshal come and take my chest of drawers, bed, and table, and leave me sittin' on a old orange crate in the middle of the room. And it come over me, mister, come over me to get mean. And I got real mean. Go down in the street and start yellin' and howlin' like a real mean woman. And the people crowd around the marshal truck and 'fore you know it that marshal turn himself around and go on back downtown empty-handed. And that's when I see it, I see the solidarity, and I start to preach it up and down. 'Cause I got me a stick and when I start poundin' time with this stick, a whole lot of people starts to march, keepin' time. We shall not be moved, yeah, we shall in no wise be disturbed. Some days I goes to court with my briefcase, raise hell with the judges. Ever time I goes into court the cops commence to holler, 'Here comes that old lawyer woman!' But all I got in here is some tore-up newspaper and a bag of cayenne pepper. Case any cop start musclin' me around – that's hot pepper, that's hot cayenne pepper. And if the judge happen to be Catholic I got my rosary layin' in there and I kind of let that crucifix hang out so's they think I'm Catholic too . . .

LUCY (*enters with milk*). Irene!

IRENE. Give it here, Lucy. Now drink it slow, mister.

Slow, slow . . . (BUSH *is drinking in sips. People now go back into themselves, read papers, stare ahead.*)

RYAN. Lee Baum! (LEE *hurries to* MOE.)

LEE. Here! Okay, Dad, let's go. (LEE *and* MOE *go to* RYAN'S *desk.*)

RYAN. This your father?

MOE. Yes.

RYAN (*to* MOE). Where's he living now?

LEE. I don't live at home because –

RYAN. Let *him* answer. Where's he living, Mr Baum?

MOE. Well he . . . he rents a room someplace.

RYAN. You gonna sit there and tell me you won't let him in the house?

MOE (*with great difficulty*). I won't let him, no.

RYAN. You mean you're the kind of man, if he rang the bell and you opened the door and saw him, you wouldn't let him inside?

MOE. Well, naturally, if he just wants to come in the house –

LEE. I don't want to live there –

RYAN. I don't care what *you* want, fella. (*To* MOE.) You will let him into the house, right?

MOE (*stiffening*). . . . . I can't stand the sight of him.

RYAN. Why I saw you both sitting here talking together the last two hours.

MOE. We weren't talking . . . We were arguing, fighting! . . .

RYAN. Fighting about what?

MOE (*despite himself growing indignant*). Who can remember? We were fighting, we're always fighting! . . .

RYAN. Look, Mr Baum . . . you're employed, aren't you?

MOE. I'm employed? Sure I'm employed. Here. (*Holds up the folded Times.*) See. Read it yourself. R. H. Macy, right? Ladies' full-length slip, genuine Japanese silk, hand-embroidered with lace top and trimmings, two ninety-eight. My boss makes four cents on these, I make a tenth of a cent. That's how I'm employed!

RYAN. You'll let him in the house. (*He starts to move.*)

MOE. I will not let him in the house! He ... he don't believe in anything! (LEE *and* RYAN *look at* MOE *in surprise, and* MOE *himself is caught off-balance by his outburst. He goes.* RYAN *glances at* LEE, *stamps a requisition form and hands it to him, convinced.*)

LEE. Thank you. (*Turns front. The welfare clients go, the row of overheard lights flies out, and only the table remains. Light up on* EDIE. *She is at an easel.* LEE *in spotlight. To audience.*) Any girl with an apartment of her own was beautiful. She made thirty-six dollars a week. She was one of the dialogue writers for the *Superman* comic strip. Edie, can I sleep here?

EDIE. Oh, hi, Lee – yeah, sure. Let me finish and I'll put a sheet on the couch. If you have any laundry throw it in the sink. I'm going to wash later. (*He stands behind her as she works.*) This is going to be a terrific sequence.

LEE. It's amazing to me how you can keep your mind on it.

EDIE. Why! Superman is one of the greatest teachers of class consciousness.

LEE. Really?

EDIE. Of course. He stands for justice. You can't have justice under capitalism, so the implications are terrific.

LEE. You're beautiful when you talk about politics, you know that? Your face gets an emanation –

EDIE (*smiling*). Don't be such a bourgeois horse's ass.

LEE. Edie, can I sleep in your bed tonight?

EDIE. Where'd you get an idea like that?

LEE. I'm lonely.

EDIE. Why don't you join the Party, for God's sake?

LEE. Aren't you lonely?

EDIE (*flushing*). I don't have to go to bed with people to be connected to mankind.

LEE. Forget I said that, will you? I'm ashamed of myself.

EDIE. I don't understand how a person who knows Marxism can hold aloof from the struggle. You're lonely because you refuse to be part of history. Why don't you join the Party?

LEE. . . . I guess I don't want to ruin my chances; I want to be a sportswriter.

EDIE. Well maybe you could write for the *Worker* sports page.

LEE. The *Daily Worker* sports page? It's a joke.

EDIE. Then help improve it.

LEE. Tell me the truth. You really think this country can go socialist?

EDIE. Where have you been? We're living in the middle of the greatest leap in class consciousness that's ever happened. Hundreds of people are joining the Party every week! Why are you so goddamn defeatist?

LEE. I was in Flint, Michigan, when the sit-down strikes started. I thought I'd write a feature story, try to sell it. It was a very confusing experience. The solidarity was enough to bring tears to your eyes. But I interviewed about thirty of them afterwards. You ought to talk to them.

EDIE. Well they're still backward. I know that.

LEE. They're not backward, they're normal. Normally anti-Semitic, anti-Negro, and anti-Soviet. They're building unions and that's good, but inside their heads it's full of fascism.

EDIE. How can you say a thing like that?

LEE. I talked to thirty men, Edie, and I found one who even knew what socialism was. There's an openly fascist organisation in Detroit – the Knights of the White Camellia –

EDIE. I know that –

LEE. It's full of auto workers. All I mean is – I'm afraid there isn't going to be time to save this country. I mean – you're afraid too, aren't you? Or are you?

EDIE. You really want my answer?

LEE. I do, yes.

EDIE. Tomorrow we're picketing the Italian consulate; Mussolini's sending Italian troops into the Spanish civil war. Come. Do something. You love Hemingway so much, read what he just said. 'One man alone is no fucking good.' As decadent as he is, even he's learning. If you want to be any good you've got to believe. It really is the final conflict, like the song says. They're fighting it out in Spain and they're going to win; the German workers are going to rise up any day now and destroy Nazism . . .

LEE. Your face gets so beautiful when you –

EDIE. Anyone can be beautiful if what they believe is beautiful. I believe in my comrades. I believe in the Soviet Union. I believe in the victory of the working class here and everywhere, and I believe in the peace that will come to the world when the people take power.

LEE. . . . But what about now, Edie?

EDIE. Now doesn't matter. The future matters! (*She removes her hand from his and limps to her writing table.*) I've got to finish this strip. I'll make up the couch in a minute.

LEE. You're a marvellous girl, Edie. Now that I'm on relief I'll take you out to dinner. – I'll pay, I mean.

EDIE (*smiles*). You are something. Why must you pay for me just because I'm a woman?

LEE. Right. I forgot about that. (*He stands. She works. He saunters up behind her and looks at her work.*) Why don't you have Superman get laid? Or married even?

EDIE. He's too busy. (*She laughs softly as she works, and he suddenly leans down to kiss her, turning her face. She starts to respond, then pushes his hand away.*) What are you doing! (*He looks down at her, nonplussed. She seems about to weep, angry and flying apart.*) I thought you were a serious person! (*She stands.*)

LEE. You suddenly looked so beautiful . . .

EDIE. But you don't want me! Why do you make everything trivial? You have no real faith in anything, do you?

LEE. Must I agree with everything you believe before I can —

EDIE. Yes! It is all one thing. Everything is connected. The same cynicism you look at the auto workers with lets you pretend to have a serious conversation when all you want is to jump into my bed.

LEE. I can't see the connection between the auto workers and —

EDIE. I have to ask you not to sleep here.

LEE. Edie, because I don't go along with all your ideas, is that —

EDIE. I'm asking you to leave. You are not a good person! (*She bursts into tears, gets up, and goes into the dark.* LEE *turns front.*)

LEE. Dear Mother. Greetings from Lake Champlain! I got paid today and I am wallowing in WPA luxury. I bought a wool shirt and a pair of warm gloves — it's already pretty cold up here. But it's so pure up here

you can get drunk breathing. The job is really wonderful; we are researching this whole section of New York
state for a sort of intimate historical guide which the
WPA is doing for every region of the country. I've been
interviewing direct descendants of soldiers who were in
the Battle of Fort Ticonderoga during the Revolution.
They all send their love. Sorry you still miss the piano
but as you say no use looking back. See you in a couple
of months. Sincerely, Lee. P.S. I assume you're the
one who put the ten-dollar bill in my jacket pocket.
*Are* things better? Please tell me the truth. (*During the
above,* ROSE *has entered and sat at the table shuffling
cards. Then enter* GRANDPA, *her niece* LUCILLE, *her
sister* FANNY, *and* DORIS, *wearing a bathrobe. They
carry chairs, sit around the table and play cards.*
GRANDPA *reads his paper.*)

ROSE. You're wearing out your bathrobe, Doris – why
don't you ever get dressed?

DORIS. Well, we only live around the corner.

ROSE. You're so young and you hardly leave the block.

DORIS. Sidney really wants me to get my high school
diploma!

ROSE. But first you'll have to get dressed.

LEE. Those long Julys in the Brooklyn neighbourhoods!
The owlish smell of the attic seeping down the stairs,
as the little house baked in the heat. Dreaming at cards
they were waiting it out where nothing any longer
seemed to move in the streets. And in the back of the
mind was always the doorbell – who could it be but a
hobo or bill collector? From Coney to Brooklyn Bridge
the cards in their thousands snapped in the silences.
(LEE *goes.* FANNY *brushes something off her chest as she
stares at the cards.*)

ROSE. Concentrate – forget your dandruff for a minute. (*The others laugh.*)

FANNY (*laughing but piqued*). It's not dandruff! It was a thread.

ROSE. *Her* dandruff is threads. (*To* LUCILLE.) Your mother!

LUCILLE. You know what she actually asked me and my sisters to do . . .?

FANNY. What's so terrible!

LUCILLE. To come over and spend the afternoon cleaning her house!

FANNY. What is so wrong? We had the most marvellous times when you were growing up – the four of us just cleaning and cleaning.

ROSE. It's an obsession.

FANNY (*mops her face*). It's really getting like an oven in here, Rose . . .

LUCILLE. I'm going to faint.

ROSE. Don't faint, all the windows are open in the back of the house. We're supposed to be away.

FANNY. But there's no draught. – For Papa's sake . . .

LUCILLE. Why couldn't you be away and you left a window open? . . . Just don't answer the door.

ROSE. I don't want to take the chance. This one is a professional collector, I've seen him do it; if a window's open he tries to listen. They're merciless . . . I sent Stanislaus for lemons, we'll have cold lemonade. Play . . .

FANNY. I can't believe they'd actually put you out, Rose.

ROSE. You can't? Wake up, Fanny, you can't be so sweet anymore – it's a bank – may they choke after the fortune of money we kept in there all those years! Ask them for two hundred dollars now and they . . . (*Tears start to her eyes.*)

FANNY. Rose, dear, come on – something'll happen, you'll see. Moe's got to find something soon, a man so well-known . . .

ROSE. I wouldn't mind so much if we hadn't been so stupid! He builds a marvellous business like that and lets a bunch of idiot brothers suck him dry.

LUCILLE. Couldn't he ask his mother for a little? . . .

ROSE. His mother says there's a Depression going on. Meantime you can go blind from the diamonds on her fingers. Which he gave her! The rottenness of people! – I tell you, the next time I start believing in anybody or anything I hope my tongue is cut out!

DORIS. Maybe Lee should come back and help out?

ROSE. Never! Lee is going to think his own thoughts and face the facts. He's got nothing to learn from us. Let him help himself.

LUCILLE. But to take up Communism –

ROSE. Lucille, what do you know about it? What does anybody know about it? The newspapers? The newspapers said the stock market will never again come down.

LUCILLE. But they're against God, Aunt Rose.

ROSE. I'm overjoyed you got so religious, Lucille, but please for God's sake don't tell me about it again!

FANNY (*rises, starts to leave*). I'll be right down.

ROSE. Now she's going to pee on her finger for luck.

FANNY. All right! So I won't go! (*She returns to her chair.*)

ROSE. So what're we playing, Doris? – cards or statues? (DORIS *sits before her cards, full of confusion.*)

GRANDPA (*putting down his paper*). Why do they need this election?

ROSE. What do you mean, why they need this election?

GRANDPA. But everybody knows Roosevelt is going to

win again. I still think he's too radical, but to go through another election is a terrible waste of money.

ROSE. What are you talking about, Papa – it's four years, they have to have an election.

GRANDPA. Why! – If they decided to make him king . . .

ROSE. King!

FANNY (*pointing at* GRANDPA, *laughing*). Believe me!

GRANDPA. If he was king he wouldn't have to waste all his time making these ridiculous election speeches and maybe he could start to improve things!

ROSE. If I had a stamp I'd write him a letter.

GRANDPA. He could be another Kaiser Franz Joseph. And the whole country would get quiet. Then after he dies you can have all the elections you want.

ROSE (*to* DORIS). Are you playing cards or hatching an egg?

DORIS (*startled*). Oh, it's my turn? (*Turns a card.*) All right; here!

ROSE. Hallelujah. (*She plays a card. It is* LUCILLE'*s turn; she plays.*) Did you lose weight?

LUCILLE. I've been trying. I'm thinking of going back to the carnival. (DORIS *quickly throws an anxious look towards* GRANDPA, *who is oblivious, reading.*)

FANNY (*indicating* GRANDPA *secretively*). You better not mention . . .

LUCILLE. He doesn't have to know, and anyway I would never dance anymore; I'd only assist the magician and tell a few jokes. They're talking about starting up again in Jersey.

ROSE. Herby can't find anything?

LUCILLE. He's going out of his mind, Aunt Rose.

ROSE. Godalmighty. So what's it going to be, Fanny?

FANNY (*feeling rushed, studying her cards*). One second! Just let me figure it out.

ROSE. When they passed around the brains this family was out to lunch. (*She gets up, unnerved, goes to a point, and is halted by . . .*)

FANNY. It's so hot in here I can't think.

ROSE. Play! I can't open the window. I'm not going to face that man again. He has merciless eyes. (STANIS-LAUS *enters from left – the front door. A middle-aged seaman in T-shirt and dungarees.*) You come in the front door? The mortgage man could come today!

STANISLAUS. I forgot! I didn't see anybody on the street, though. (*Lifts bag of lemons.*) Fresh lemonade coming up on deck. (*He crosses.*) I starched all the napkins. (*He goes.*)

ROSE. Starched all the napkins . . . they're cracking like matzos. I feel like doing a fortune. (*Takes out another deck of cards, lays out a fortune.*)

LUCILLE. I don't know, Aunt Rose, is it so smart to let this man live with you?

DORIS. I would never dare! How can you sleep at night with a strange man in the cellar?

FANNY. Nooo! Stanislaus is a gentleman. (*To* ROSE.) I think he's a little bit a fairy, isn't he?

ROSE. I hope! (*They all laugh.*) For God's sake, Fanny, play the queen of clubs!

FANNY. How did you know I had the queen of clubs!

ROSE. Because I'm smart, I voted for Herbert Hoover. – I see what's been played, dear, so I figure what's left.

FANNY (*to* GRANDPA, *who continues reading*). She's a marvel, she's got Grandma's head.

ROSE. Huh! – Look at this fortune.

FANNY. Here, I'm playing. (*Plays a card.*)

ROSE (*continuing to lay out the fortune*). I always feed them on the porch, but when I hand him a plate of soup he says he wants to wash the windows before he

eats. *Before!* That I never heard. I nearly fell over. Go
ahead, Doris, it's you.

DORIS (*desperately trying to be quick*). I know just what to
do, wait a minute. (*The women freeze, study their cards;*
ROSE *now faces front. She is quickly isolated in light.*)

ROSE. When I went to school we had to sit like soldiers,
with backs straight and our hands clasped on the desk;
things were supposed to be upright. When the navy
came up the Hudson River, you cried it was so beautiful. You even cried when they shot the Czar of Russia.
He was also beautiful. President Warren Gamaliel
Harding, another beauty. Mayor James J. Walker
smiled like an angel, what a nose, and tiny feet. Richard
Whitney, president of the Stock Exchange, a handsome, upright man. I could name a hundred from the
rotogravure! Who could know that these upright handsome men would either turn out to be crooks who
would land in jail or ignoramuses? What is left to believe? The bathroom. I lock myself in and hold onto
the faucets so I shouldn't scream. At my husband, my
mother-in-law, at God knows what until they take me
away . . . (*Returning to the fortune and with deep
anxiety.*) What the hell did I lay out here? What is
this? (*Light returns to normal.*)

DORIS. 'Gray's Elegy in the Country Churchyard.'

ROSE. What?

FANNY (*touching her arm worriedly*). Why don't you lie
down, Rose? . . .

ROSE. Lie down . . . why? (*To* DORIS.) What Gray's
'Elegy'? What are you? . . . (STANISLAUS *enters rapidly
– wearing a waist-length, white starched waiter's jacket,
a tray expertly on his shoulder on which are glasses, and
rolled napkins. Rose shows alarmed expression as she lays
a card down on the fortune.*)

STANISLAUS. It's a braw bricht moonlicht nicht tonicht
– that's Scotch.

FANNY. How does he get those napkins to stand up!

ROSE (*under terrific tension – she tears her gaze from the
cards she laid out*). What's the jacket suddenly? (*The
women watch her tensely.*)

STANISLAUS. S.S. Manhattan. Captain's steward at your
service. (*Salutes.*)

ROSE. Will you stop this nightmare? Take that jacket off.
What're you talking about, captain's steward? Who are
you?

STANISLAUS. I was captain's personal steward, but
they're not sailing the Manhattan anymore. Served J.
Pierpont Morgan, John D. Rockefeller, Enrico Caruso,
Lionel –

ROSE (*very suspiciously*). Bring in the cookies, please. (*He
picks up the pitcher to pour the lemonade.*) Thank you,
I'll pour it. Go, please. (*She doesn't look at him; he goes
out. In the silence she picks up the pitcher, tilts it, but her
hand is shaking and* FANNY *takes the pitcher.*)

FANNY. Rose, dear, come upstairs . . .

ROSE. How does he look to you?

FANNY. Why? He looks very nice.

LUCILLE. He certainly keeps the house beautiful, Aunt
Rose, it's like a ship.

ROSE. He's a liar, though; anything comes into his head,
he says; what am I believing him for? What the hell got
into me? You can tell he's full of shit and he comes to
the door, a perfect stranger, and I let him sleep in the
cellar!

LUCILLE. Shh! (STANISLAUS *enters with a plate of
cookies, in T-shirt again, determinedly . . .*)

ROSE. Listen, Stanislaus . . . (*She stands.*)

STANISLAUS (*he senses his imminent dismissal*). I go down

to the ship chandler store tomorrow, get some special white paint, paint the whole outside the house. I got plenty of credit, don't cost you.

ROSE. I thought it over, you understand?

STANISLAUS (*with a desperate smile*). I borrow big ladder from the hardware store. And I gonna make nice curtains for the cellar windows. Excuse me, gotta clean out icebox. Taste the lemonade, I learn that in Spanish submarine. (*He gets himself out.*)

FANNY. I think he's very sweet, Rose . . . Here . . . (*Offers a glass of lemonade.*)

LUCILLE. Don't worry about that mortgage man, Aunt Rose, it's after five, they don't come after five . . .

ROSE (*caught in her uncertainty*). He seems sweet to you?

GRANDPA (*putting the paper down*). What Lee ought to do . . . Rosie?

ROSE. Hah?

GRANDPA. Lee should go to Russia. (*The sisters and* LUCILLE *turn to him in surprise.*)

ROSE (*incredulous, frightened*). To Russia?

GRANDPA. In Russia they need everything; whereas here, y'see, they don't need anything, so therefore, there's no work.

ROSE (*with an edge of hysteria*). Five minutes ago Roosevelt is too radical, and now you're sending Lee to Russia?

GRANDPA. That's different. Look what it says here . . . a hundred thousand American people applying for jobs in Russia. Look, it says it. So if Lee would go over there and open up a nice chain of clothing stores –

ROSE. Papa! You're such a big anti-Communist . . . And you don't know the government owns everything in Russia?

GRANDPA. Yeah, but not the *stores*.

ROSE. Of course the stores!

GRANDPA. The *stores* they own?

ROSE. Yes!

GRANDPA. Them bastards.

ROSE (*to* LUCILLE). I'll go out of my mind here . . .

DORIS. So who wrote it?

ROSE. Wrote what?

DORIS. 'Gray's Elegy in a Country Churchyard.' It was a fifteen-dollar question on the radio yesterday, but you were out. I ran to call you.

ROSE. Who wrote Gray's 'Elegy in a Country Church-yard'?

DORIS. By the time I got back to the radio it was another question.

ROSE. Doris, darling . . . (*Slowly.*) Gray's 'Elegy in a' – (FANNY *laughs.*) What are you laughing at, do you know?

FANNY (*pleasantly*). How would I know?

LUCILLE. Is it Gray? (ROSE *looks at her, an enormous sadness in her eyes. With a certain timidity.*) Well it says 'Gray's Elegy', right?

DORIS. How could it be Gray? That's the title! (ROSE *is staring ahead in an agony of despair.*)

FANNY. What's the matter, Rose?

DORIS. Well, what'd I say?

FANNY. Rose, what's the matter?

LUCILLE. You all right?

FANNY (*really alarmed – turning* ROSE'*s face to her*). What is the matter! (ROSE *bursts into tears.* FANNY *gets up and embraces her, almost crying herself.*) Oh, Rosie, please . . . don't. It'll get better, something's got to happen . . . (*A sound from the front door – galvanizes them.*)

DORIS (*pointing off left.*). There's some –

ROSE (*her hands flying up in fury*). Sssh! (*Whispering.*) I'll go upstairs. I'm not home. (*Starts right.* MOE *enters.*)

DORIS (*laughing*). It's Uncle Moe!

MOE. What's the excitement?

ROSE (*crossing to him*). Oh, thank God, I thought it was the mortgage man. You're home early. (*He stands watching her.*)

FANNY. Let's go, come on. (*They begin to clear table of tray, lemonade, glasses, etc.*)

MOE (*looking into* ROSE's *face*). You crying?

LUCILLE. How's it in the city?

ROSE. Go out the back, huh?

MOE. The city is murder.

FANNY. Will you get your bills together? I'm going downtown tomorrow.

ROSE. Take a shower. Why are you so pale?

LUCILLE. Bye-bye, Uncle Moe.

MOE. Bye, girls.

DORIS (*as she goes with* FANNY *and* LUCILLE). I must ask him how he made that lemonade . . . (*They are gone.* MOE *is staring at some vision, quite calmly, but absorbed.*)

ROSE. You . . . sell anything? . . . No, heh? (*He shakes his head negatively – but that is not what he is thinking about.*) Here . . . (*She gets a glass from the table.*) Come drink, it's cold. (*He takes it, but doesn't drink.*)

MOE. You're hysterical every night.

ROSE. No, I'm all right. It's just all so stupid and every once in a while I can't . . . I can't . . . (*She is holding her head.*)

MOE. The thing is . . . You listening to me?

ROSE. What? (*Suddenly aware of her father's pressure on* MOE, *turns and goes quickly to him.*) Go on the back porch, Papa, huh? It's shady there now . . . (*She hands him a glass of lemonade.*)

GRANDPA. But the man'll see me.

ROSE. It's all right, he won't come so late, and Moe is here. Go . . . (GRANDPA *is moving upstage*.) . . . And why don't you put on your other glasses, they're much cooler. (GRANDPA *is gone. She returns to* MOE.) Yes, dear. What. What's going to be?

MOE. We are going to be all right.

ROSE. Why?

MOE. Because we are. So this nervousness every night is unnecessary and I wish to God –

ROSE (*indicating the table and the cards spread out*). It's just a fortune. I . . . I started to do a fortune, and I saw . . . a young man. The death of a young man.

MOE (*struck*). You don't say.

ROSE (*sensing*). Why? (*He turns front, amazed, frightened*.) Why'd you say that!

MOE. Nothing . . .

ROSE. Is Lee? . . .

MOE. Will you cut that out –

ROSE. Tell me!

MOE. I saw a terrible thing on the subway. Somebody jumped in front of a train.

ROSE. Aaaahhh – again! My God! You saw him?

MOE. No, a few minutes before I got there. Seems he was a very young man. One of the policemen was holding a great big basket of flowers. Seems he was trying to sell flowers.

ROSE. I saw it! (*Her spine tingling, pointing down at the cards*.) Look, it's there! I'm going to write to Lee to come home immediately. I want you to put in that you want him home.

MOE. I have nothing for him, Rose; how can I make him come home?

ROSE (*screaming and weeping*). Then go to your mother

and stand up like a man to her . . . instead of this god-damned fool! (*She weeps.*)

MOE (*stung, nearly beaten – not facing her*). This can't . . . it can't go on forever, Rose, a country can't just die! (*She goes on weeping; he cries out in pain.*) Will you stop? I'm trying! Godalmighty, I am trying! (*The doorbell rings. They start with shock, she facing left, he only half-turned toward the sound.* GRANDPA *enters hurrying, pointing left.*)

GRANDPA. Rose –

ROSE. Ssssh! (*The bell rings again.* MOE *presses stiffened fingers against his temple, his eyes averted in humiliation. Whispering.*) God in heaven . . . make him go away! (*The bell rings again.* MOE's *head is bent, his hand quivering as it grips his forehead.*) Oh, dear God, give our new President the strength, and the wisdom . . . (*Doorbell rings, a little more insistently.*) . . . give Mr Roosevelt the way to help us . . . (*Doorbell.*) Oh, my God, help our dear country . . . and the people! . . . (*The doorbell rings unceasingly now as the lights lower. The sound of a sports crowd. Light on* LEE, *finishing his notes at ringside.* SIDNEY *in a guard's uniform appears. Both are grey-haired. Elements of a fight ring in background.*)

SIDNEY. Good fight tonight, Mr Baum.

LEE. Huh? It was all right.

SIDNEY. Pardon me bothering you, but I enjoy your column a lot.

LEE. Oh? Thanks very much. (*Starts to pass him.*)

SIDNEY (*finally coming out with it*). Hey!

LEE (*surprised by the impertinence*). Huh? (*Recognises him now.*) Sidney! Good God, Sidney!

SIDNEY. Boy, you're some cousin. I'm looking straight at you and no recognito!

LEE. Well I've never seen you in that uniform.

SIDNEY. I'm Chief of Uniformed Security here.

LEE. Great!

SIDNEY. I was surprised you were covering the fight tonight.

LEE. I decided to get back to my column again – Did I hear your mother died?

SIDNEY. Yep, she's gone – I was sorry to hear about Aunt Rose . . . and Moe.

VOICE (*off*). Takin' 'em out, Sidney!

SIDNEY (*calls off*). Yeah, okay. (*Spotlights over the ring go out.*)

LEE. And you are Doris are? . . .

SIDNEY. Oh yeah, we're practically the only ones we know who didn't get divorced. You know who'd love to see you? Remember Lou Charney?

LEE. Charney.

SIDNEY. On the track team, you remember – you and him used to trot to school together every morning.

LEE (*still not sure, but*). Oh yeah, Lou – how is he?

SIDNEY. He's dead – he got killed in Italy in the war . . . but his mother still talks about you and him trotting off together every morning . . .

LEE. Really . . . and who lives in our house?

SIDNEY. Puerto Rican FBI man. Nice people, but they never mow. (*Holds out hand knee-high.*) You knew Georgie Rosen got killed, didn't you?

LEE. Georgie Rosen.

SIDNEY (*holds hand out very low*). Little Georgie – sold you his racing bike, I think.

LEE (*recalling now*). Georgie too!

SIDNEY (*nodding happily*). Plenty of wars on that block.

LEE (*shakes his head*). – You look good, Sidney.

SIDNEY. You too. – It's a different country, though, huh?

LEE. How do you mean?

SIDNEY. I don't know – the attitudes, and all. But I can't help it – I guess I'm hooked on this country – I still look forward! Still keep waiting for the good news! – You probably think I'm crazy . . .

LEE. No, why should I?

SIDNEY (*grasps* LEE's *arm gratefully*). You're that way too, right?

LEE. . . . I'm afraid so.

SIDNEY. I knew it! – Come on, Lee, let me drop you – I've got a car in the garage. – Can I buy you a drink?

LEE. Great!

SIDNEY. Listen, I'll send you a tape of my last song? – I call it 'A Moon of My Own'. Nice title, you think?

LEE. Yeah, that sounds terrific. (SIDNEY *is vanishing into darkness*.)

SIDNEY. 'A Moon of My Own' – suddenly came to me when I was sitting on the porch . . . (SIDNEY *goes into darkness, but* LEE *remains behind. And light rises, hazy and dim, on* ROSE *at the piano, very softly playing in an abnormally slow tempo that seems to come across a vast distance.* LEE *is in sharp white light.*)

LEE. After all these years I still can't settle with myself about my mother. In her own crazy way she was so much like the country. There was nothing she believed that she didn't also believe the opposite. She'd sit down on the subway next to a black man and in a couple of minutes she had him confiding some very intimate things in his life. Then, maybe a day later – (*Alarmed.*) 'Did you hear! They say the coloured are moving in!' Or she'd lament her fate as a woman: 'I was born twenty years too soon,' she'd say. 'They treated a

woman like a cow, fill her up with a baby and lock her
in for the rest of her life.' But then she'd warn me,
'Watch out for women – when they're not stupid
they're full of deceit.' I'd come home and give her a
real bath of radical idealism and she was ready to storm
the barricades; by evening she'd fallen in love again
with the Prince of Wales. She was so like the country;
money obsessed her but what she really longed for was
some kind of height where she could stand and see out
and around and breathe in the air of her own free life.
With all her defeats she believed to the end that the
world was meant to be better. – I don't know; all I
know for sure whenever I think of her is that I always
end up – with this headful of life!

ROSE (*at piano*). Sing! (*He grins, turns quickly to her;
she is far off in the distance, hands beckoning to him
over the keyboard. As bright light flashes over the
cloud-covered continent in the background ... He
walks towards her and lights lower to dark on them both,
as* ROBERTSON *appears – in his seventies, with his
cane.*)

ROBERTSON. Interviewers always ask the same two
questions – could it happen again, is the first. I cannot
get myself to believe that we would allow the whole
economy to disintegrate again, but of course there is no
limit to human stupidity. The second question is
whether it was really Roosevelt who saved the country.
(*Pause.*) In truth, he was a conservative, traditional man
who was driven to the Left by one emergency after
another. There were moments when the word Revolution was not regarded as rhetoric. But willy-nilly, the
net result of all his floundering, his experimentation,
his truth-telling and his dire prevarications – was that
the people came to believe that the country actually

belonged to them. I'm not at all sure that this was his intention; I'm not even certain exactly how it came to be, but in my opinion – that belief is what saved the United States.

*Blackout.*

## Methuen's Modern Plays

| | |
|---|---|
| Jean Anouilh | *Antigone* |
| | *Becket* |
| | *The Lark* |
| John Arden | *Serjeant Musgrave's Dance* |
| | *The Workhouse Donkey* |
| | *Armstrong's Last Goodnight* |
| John Arden and | *The Business of Good Government* |
| Margaretta D'Arcy | *The Royal Pardon* |
| | *The Hero Rises Up* |
| | *The Island of the Mighty* |
| | *Vandaleur's Folly* |
| Wolfgang Bauer, | *Shakespeare the Sadist* |
| Rainer Werner | |
|    Fassbinder, | *Bremen Coffee,* |
| Peter Handke, | *My Foot My Tutor,* |
| Frank Xaver Kroetz | *Stallerhof* |
| Brendan Behan | *The Quare Fellow* |
| | *The Hostage* |
| | *Richard's Cork Leg* |
| Edward Bond | *A-A-America!* and *Stone* |
| | *Saved* |
| | *Narrow Road to the Deep North* |
| | *The Pope's Wedding* |
| | *Lear* |
| | *The Sea* |
| | *Bingo* |
| | *The Fool* and *We Come to the River* |
| | *Theatre Poems and Songs* |
| | *The Bundle* |
| | *The Woman* |
| | *The Worlds* with *The Activists Papers* |
| | *Restoration* and *The Cat* |
| | *Summer* and *Fables* |
| Bertolt Brecht | *Mother Courage and Her Children* |
| | *The Caucasian Chalk Circle* |
| | *The Good Person of Szechwan* |
| | *The Life of Galileo* |
| | *The Threepenny Opera* |
| | *Saint Joan of the Stockyards* |
| | *The Resistible Rise of Arturo Ui* |
| | *The Mother* |
| | *Mr Puntila and His Man Matti* |
| | *The Measures Taken and other* |
| |    *Lehrstücke* |
| | *The Days of the Commune* |

| | |
|---|---|
| Kaufman and Hart | *Once in a Lifetime, You Can't Take It With You* and *The Man Who Came To Dinner* |
| Barrie Keeffe | *Gimme Shelter (Gem, Gotcha, Getaway)* |
| | *Barbarians (Killing Time, Abide With Me, In the City)* |
| | *A Mad World, My Masters* |
| Arthur Kopit | *Indians* |
| | *Wings* |
| John McGrath | *The Cheviot, the Stag and the Black, Black Oil* |
| David Mercer | *After Haggerty* |
| | *The Bankrupt and other plays* |
| | *Cousin Vladimir* and *Shooting the Chandelier* |
| | *Duck Song* |
| | *The Monster of Karlovy Vary* and *Then and Now* |
| | *No Limits To Love* |
| Arthur Miller | *The American Clock* |
| Peter Nichols | *Passion Play* |
| | *Poppy* |
| Joe Orton | *Loot* |
| | *What the Butler Saw* |
| | *Funeral Games* and *The Good and Faithful Servant* |
| | *Entertaining Mr Sloane* |
| | *Up Against It* |
| Harold Pinter | *The Birthday Party* |
| | *The Room* and *The Dumb Waiter* |
| | *The Caretaker* |
| | *A Slight Ache and other plays* |
| | *The Collection* and *The Lover* |
| | *The Homecoming* |
| | *Tea Party and other plays* |
| | *Landscape and Silence* |
| | *Old Times* |
| | *No Man's Land* |
| | *Betrayal* |
| | *The Hothouse* |
| | *Other Places (A Kind of Alaska, Victoria Station, Family Voices)* |
| Luigi Pirandello | *Henry IV* |
| | *Six Characters in Search of an Author* |
| Stephen Poliakoff | *Hitting Town* and *City Sugar* |
| David Rudkin | *The Sons of Light* |
| | *The Triumph of Death* |

*If you would like to receive, free of charge, regular information about new plays and theatre books from Methuen, please send your name and address to:*

The Marketing Department (Drama)
Methuen London Ltd
North Way
Andover
Hampshire SP10 5BE